Incubated in China

Incubated in China

a memoir

"with an almost scaring honesty"

SHUBILA RUTH KIKOKO

INCUBATED IN CHINA. Copyright © 2016 by Shubila Ruth Kikoko. All rights reserved. No parts of this book may be used or reproduced in any manner whatsoever without written permission except in the case of brief quotations embodied in critical articles and reviews. For information, please email: 2487167293@qq.com

ISBN: 978-1-78280-848-0

DEDICATION

To my parents, Eng. Hassan and Ruth Kikoko, the love and foundation that you have provided in the lives of my siblings and I, is immeasurable. You have set a great example, a high standard on what it means to be parents. I hope that your grandchildren and great grandchildren will get to understand what kind of people you were and draw strength from that, as we have.

Mama Nasra, we love you! You are an important part of our family. We appreciate your love and companionship to our dad till his death.

To my siblings, Siima, Ibrahim and Nasra. I cannot imagine this journey of life without your presence. You have been a blessing to me in more ways than you can imagine or that I can explain. I want you to always be happy and to experience fullness of joy in your lives. Always know that my soul loves you guys with no reservations.

Deogratius my darling, I bless God's name every time I think about us. You are perfect in so many ways that I get overwhelmed knowing that you are a direct communication from God – answering my prayers. I'm a forever grateful for your immense and solid support. We are going to have adventures you and me. Amen!

CONTENTS

APPRECIATION FOR WUHAN CITY
PREFACE
INTRODUCTION 1
1. THE GENESIS 7
   Good Student Syndrome 9
   Sexual Corruption 13
   Post Undergraduate Graduation 19
   Ambition Retardation 22

2. WHY CHINA? SAYING GOODBYE 29
   Corporate World 31
   Why China? 35
   The Plan 42

3. LUOSHI ROAD – EARLY CHALLENGES 45
   The Power Of Your Mind 47
   Racial Challenges 50
   From a Corporate Exec to Installing hair extensions 55
   When They Give You a Chance! 60
   No Shame 64

4. BETTER THAN YESTERDAY 69
   A Cussing Brainy? 71
   Being Sad Is A Sin 73
   Do Better 76

5. STILLNESSS 81
   Forgiveness 83
   Thin Line To Insanity 86
   Self – Disciplining 88

6. PATH TO LOVE 95
   Past Relationships.. 97
   Meeting My love 108

7. DAD'S PASSING 115
   Dream Came True.. 117
   A Peaceful Death.. 120
   Life Is Nothing But A Moment 125

8. MOM AND DAD – LESSONS LEARNT...................... 129
   Unshakable faith 131
   Obedience to God... 135
   Sacrifice 146
   Unconditional Love 149
   Confidence.. 152
   Sense Of Humor.. 159

9. CHARITY WORKS 165
   Spiritual Attack.. 167
   Soul Conviction 170
   Ideas On Philanthropy 174

10. ITS NOT ENOUGH, THIS IS ENOUGH!.................... 177
    New Ventures 179
    Being your own brand 183
    Why Not You? 188
ACKNOWLEDGMENTS 195

APPRECIATION FOR WUHAN CITY

Before I left Tanzania in September 2011, I used to think that Tanzanians were the most hospitable people in the world. But my goodness! Wait till you meet the Chinese. Whenever I was out with friends, paying the bill was often overwhelming. I once had a long discussion with my English student. And the argument was that he should agree to share the bill after we had a meal together. We were both students at Wuhan University of Technology at the time. But it didn't matter to him. He still wanted to pay for dinner for the sake of being hospitable.

Wuhan has more higher education institutions than any other city in the world with about 80 universities. And it is ranked 11th on a list of the World Most Dynamic Cities of 2025 on the American 'Foreign policy' magazine.[1] It is located in central China with a population of about 10 million people. It is my second home. The city is full of colors and life, especially during festivals when there are red lanterns and night lights everywhere. It is very beautiful. And the people are very humble. You can meet a

---

[1] WNLO_POEM, 2015. The Rise of a Great City. Available online: ttp://wxphp.com/wxd_9zl1t8wwxy3sk4u08kjh_1.html

Chinese who is excellent in what he does, but when you compliment him, that is when you learn what it means to be modest. At first, I used to insist, "I mean it, you are very good," I would say. But my friend wouldn't accept the compliment. He kept on saying, "Oh no, not really." I later I found out that's how the Chinese respond to praises.

If somebody told me when I first arrived in China that I would one day understand Putonghua (also known as Mandarin) – the official language in China – even a little or speak some of the words with such an ease without even searching for the words in my mind, I wouldn't agree. Having spent five years in Wuhan, I have made history and beautiful memories there. I have made an attachment with different streets and avenues. I remember visiting the famous Han Street (known as 'Hanjie' in Mandarin with two of my friends, Gnougoussa and Thomas, who were also pursuing an MBA at the University. I passed by that area the other day in a taxi and it was as though I could see us three goofing around and taking photos. Although it is almost just five years, it feels longer, like I have lived in Wuhan for many years.

I have beautiful memories in my mind of that place. I remember once when I was in Huangpi, a rural district 50 kilometers north of Wuhan, I had an interesting encounter with a local taxi driver. He was an old man and he asked where I am from. When he learnt that I was from Tanzania, he refused to accept my money. He said that Tanzania and China has a good relationship. I was happy but surprised since I know how the Chinese are with money. For example, in the shops they wouldn't sell something to you if you are just 5 cents (5 mao) short. Since then, whenever I took a taxi, I mentioned that I was from Tanzania. But it never again worked in my favor.

I remember a Chinese man who had returned to Wuhan from Singapore, to open an education centre. We met at a fundraising event in 2012, a year after I had arrived in China. He invited me for a few 'English corners' sessions, where English students would have a topic to discuss for an hour or so. He was one of the few people who accepted me as African, and gave me a chance to teach in a formal institution.

The trip I made to Hubuxiang food market with five of my students is unforgettable. We enjoyed the food, the lights, the history and some photo sessions. Three of the students who majored in art and design took awesome photos. And after the night was over, we took a bus back to Wuchang. Wuhan has three districts – Wuchang, Hankou and Hanyang. I lived in Wuchang. I remember seeing a baby in the bus, who could have been a year old. He started crying when he saw me. I think the baby didn't understand why I was black. He was used to seeing everyone around him as white or yellow. I must have scared him to death. This was hilarious. Well not on the spot, but thinking about it afterwards – it certainly was. This was a typical African woman's story in China!

The plane trees – from genus called Platanus lined up on each side of the road in one the streets of Wuhan University of Technology, Mafangshan East Campus, have a special place in my heart. In one of the last conversations I had with my late father, Hassan Kikoko, I sent him a photo of these trees. I told him that I loved them because I felt very peaceful walking under them. Every time I pass along this road, I remember my dad. They have become special to me.

I feel like Wuhan and I were destined to meet. Our first encounter was in 2009 when I had visited my best friend, Dr. Natasha Choka who was a medical student at Tongji Medical College at the time. I fell in love with the city and made plans to go back for my MBA, two years later. Now, when I pass by the university, I remember the block Natasha used to live in. I remember how we snuck between the glass doors after she picked me up from the airport. It was late and the security guard had already closed the doors of the dorm. That is another beautiful memory.

Wuhan feels like home especially when returning back after a travel to other cities. Not just myself but other international students also experience this after staying Wuhan for few years. The city has a way to welcome and charm you with its liveliness and warmth. The teachers and members of the international students office were always striving to make us (the foreign students) have a comfortable stay in Wuhan.

Prof. Yuan Guohua the Dean of International Education and my teacher – he was my favorite. He made me love Marketing even more because of his excellence and dedication to imparting knowledge on his students. My supervisor, Prof Song Yiyuan was incredibly patient with me during the passing of my father in 2015 and when I had to extend my research. I am mostly indebted to him.

The slogan: 'Wuhan different every day!' – is indeed true. We witness constructions and infrastructures being built in an amazing speed, such as the subway stations connecting all three districts of Wuhan. After its completion this made transportation very convenient, helping us escape the traffic jams while commuting in buses.

Wuhan will always have a place in my heart. I will always cherish the kind hearted, straightforward and friendly people of Wuhan. It is where I wrote my first book, where I had a quiet time to grow in my character and spiritual life.

PREFACE

What do I want? – To do what is right. To do what I feel in my heart I should do. I want to glorify God. I want to be in peace with my creator. This is what I want.

I wanted to write a book since I was a teenager. Quite surprising to think of it, no one in my family was has ever written a book. It's not like I had seen anybody in my circles that inspired me. However, when my mother passed away in 1999, I thought to myself that if she had written a book on how she saw life and her fight with cancer that would have helped a lot of people. I was sixteen at the time and I promised myself that I would write about her fight and her faith in God. That's how I started aspiring to become a writer.

I have been through a lot of chaos in my life. I thought that there was no way I would go through all of that and just sit on it. I truly believe that there has to be a reason why I went through all I did. This is why I share my experience. And maybe in the process, someone will be relieved of their pain. Maybe, they will get direction in life and know that God's mercy is always there for us. All we need to do is let Him in.

I hope that through this book, the struggles, the shame, and experiences that I went through will be beneficial to someone else. I hope that it will motivate and encourage someone. In that way the Lord's name will be glorified, in all the wonderful things He has done.

I am not perfect instead every day I press on towards the mark of the high calling. This book is not about perfection at all. And if I had waited until I was perfect, I feel maybe I could have waited forever. I have realized that it's not about being perfect but making a choice to do good, becoming better and honoring that commitment every day. I must admit that while writing this book, I had doubts and fears. I worried about my image. What about people's perception of me? Will this book deter my future trajectory? Will the book bring shame to my family, my siblings, my future husband and children? How about my poor writing skills? Will I be allowed to market the book in China? Will my studies be jeopardized because of this book? This is what I told my fears;

1 Peter 3:13-14 NIV

Who is going to harm you if you are eager to do good? But even if you should suffer for what is right, you are blessed. "Do not fear their threats; do not be frightened."

Shubila Ruth Kikoko

Wuhan, China

20/10/ 2015

Incubated in China

INTRODUCTION

It was late, around 9 pm when I received a call from my laoshi [2]. On the other side, I heard, "I have some news for you. The university has changed the salary," she said. I was excited I didn't wait for her to finish. I asked, "They increased the pay?" But to my surprise she said, "No, they've cut off half of it". I was surprised. I couldn't believe this was happening. I mean, as assistant teachers, we used to be paid as per hours labored. Sometimes, we would get more than 5000 RMB (about $762) per month. Then, it was decided to reduce payment to a flat rate of 3000 RMB (about $457) per month. Now they were reducing it to 1600 RMB (about $244). This was the last quarter of 2015. I was the beginning of the last year of my PhD in Strategic Enterprise Management, before I made an extension to graduate in 2017.

Later that night, I left her a text message and also called her in the morning. I told her that I wouldn't be able to continue as her assistant. I quit. This was the second job that I had quit in a span of three months. I had three part

---

[2] Laoshi means teacher in Chinese

time jobs – internships at the time. First, I taught International Marketing at the university (this didn't pay much and I wasn't doing it for the money but for the experience). I was also an assistant teacher at the University. I interacted with students a lot and edited their reports. It consumed a lot of time. But since I was being paid according to the hours I worked, it wasn't a problem. However, a new policy emerged each semester and the salary would be less and less. The third part time job was teaching English at a private institution. My students were preparing themselves for IELTS exams. Remunerations for this was job was attractive since I would work for a lot of hours. But not until a 'white' teacher was hired, then all the students preferred to take his class. I went from 100 hours to 5 hours per month. I later quit that job also. The doors had started closing slowly, one by one. Now, I was completely convinced that God himself was in play. It was clear to me that He was letting these events happen so that I would submit (sort of putting me in a corner) and do something better with my life or that which I believe to be His will and purpose for my life.

While these things were happening, I questioned myself, *Shubi, what do you want? Why did you come to China?* I was restless. However, on the next morning after my laoshi's call, I wasn't upset anymore. I thought to myself that things were the way they were supposed to be. I laughed about it, thinking of how God's infinite wisdom was truly divine in my life. However, I will not lie at one point I was scared and I thought to myself, *What's happening? What if I am being punished by God?* – for what? I don't know. But I could see that doors were being closed one after the other.

I used to love a track by Tanzanian gospel singer, Ambwene Mwasongwe 'Tangulia mbele' (Go ahead of me). But only during this difficult time did the true meaning of this verse translated below hit home.

"An eagle builds a nest on a tree with thorns, covering them with feathers,

A time comes when the baby eagles are matured, the mother eagle denies them food so they can come out and be taught how to fly,

When they continue to refuse to come out the mother eagle takes away the feathers and the thorns will force the baby eagles to come out,

The eagles' intention is not to hurt her babies,

The eagle's goal is to teach them to fly high."

Our relationship with God is something similar. At least

that is how I viewed my situation at that point in my life. Sometimes, the positions we hold contradict the purpose of our lives according to the will of God. Maybe the job you have is just relief support. But God wants you to fly higher and not get comfortable with where you are – just like the mother eagle.

When the time comes, she teaches her babies how to fly and get off support. If we are not careful we might see the 'getting off relief support' as a negative thing. We might even want to keep on holding on to being on support. In doing so, we keep going round and round the same mountains instead of making progress. That's why it might take us years to experience victory. [3] *The Lord our God said to us in Horeb, you have dwelt long enough on this mountain.* [Deuteronomy 1:6| NIV]

I was in a place where one; I had huge expenses coming up. My fiancé, Deo and I were planning our engagement that was scheduled for February 2016. And it was already October 2015 when the major sources of income were disappearing. I was also saving for our wedding since we were both going to contribute an amount. And I had to pay for an extra year of my PhD study. I wanted to extend

---

[3] Joyce Meyer, 2011. The Battlefield Of The Mind

a year so I could get enough time to publish papers since I hadn't completed all the requirements for graduation. Two, financial doors were closing. Three, I had started to lose interest in what I was doing. I felt teaching English was not for me nor was it why I came to China. Contemplating on this position, I knew that God had cornered me and that the time had come to pursue something more meaningful. I had a good laugh thinking about this.

That morning, I decided to watch Maya Angelou interviews on YouTube. Maya, a great Black American poet, talked about having the courage to follow your dreams and how courage is the most important of all virtues. Without it, we wouldn't be able to achieve other virtues effectively. That made a lot of sense to me, it also gave me courage. My best quote from her interview was, *"I am a human being. Nothing human can be alien to me."* As long as all extraordinary things have been done by human beings then anyone can do them. So don't sell yourself short.

I also watched one of Oprah's motivational stories, and one of the things she said that touched my heart was, *"Writers write that's what they do whether 15 million or 15 people will read their book".* She continued, *"This is to allow the truth of yourself to express itself as everybody is looking for the highest fullest expression of ourselves as human beings"*

That same morning - October 10, 2015 - I started writing this book. My first of many, I hope. In pursue of what was dear to my heart since I was a teenager. I hope that it will encourage someone reading it to press forward to achieve their dreams and purpose for life. If you will be blessed by this content then all glory to God. I do not want to share the glory for this work because it is God who blessed me with an opportunity to share with you His grace and mercy to my imperfect ways. But for anything offensive, I fully take responsibility and regret for that. May God bless you!

1. THE GENESIS

But I think my mistakes became the chemistry for my miracles. I think that my tests became my testimonies.

T. D. Jakes

Good Student Syndrome

I was a good student in Primary School. I was never the top performer in class, no. But I was certainly among the best. Some teachers would speak highly of me to my siblings. We went to the same school, Muhimbili Primary School in Dar es Salaam, Tanzania. In those days, it was one of the best public schools in town.

Even before I got to Standard Seven, I would get nervous just thinking about the whole year ahead. There was a Maths teacher who was known to be very strict. He would cane students more than any teacher in the school. His name was Mwalimu Ndossi.[4] To my surprise, when I got to Standard Seven, I became his amongst his favorite students. I was among his assistants, helping him to correct other students' work after he had corrected ours (his assistants' work). That gave me a lot of confidence. But I started to notice that I was not among the cool kids nor was I regarded as one. I was small in posture, extremely neat and the teachers loved me. When I look at the pictures of myself as a teenager, I think I was almost annoying in how a 'Miss goody two shoes' I was. And

---

[4] Mwalimu means teacher in Kiswahili.

that's just what I think of myself. Imagine what other people thought of me then.

You have to understand that not everybody will like you when you are different, especially your peers. People tend to get uncomfortable with that which is different. You have to embrace being different and know that it is okay. That is what makes you you and unique.

Once I was done with primary school, I went to one of the most prestigious government girls' high schools. Up to this day, I remember when my mom came from work and told me that my name was among the students that would go to Jangwani Girls' Secondary School. I was undoubtedly very happy and excited. Why was Jangwani special? First, it was in the city, just 15 minutes' walk from my home. Back then, I really didn't imagine myself going far from home in the countryside where other best schools were located. Jangwani accepted students who passed well in Mathematics, Science and English. Also, I loved the orange colored skirt as school uniform. I thought it was cute.

I spent seven years in that high school as a day student. Only one semester during last year of Advanced level (A level) did I stay in the school's dormitory. This was to have more quality time of study, in preparation of the final exams that would lead to university.

I was a science student in my Ordinary Level (O-Level) and for my A-Level, I majored in Chemistry Biology and Nutrition (CBN). When I was in my O level, my cousin sister was also studying at Jangwani. She was in her A levels pursing Chemistry, Biology and Nutrition (CBN) as a major. She is now Dr. Grace Msoffe, after attaining her doctorate degree in South Africa. She is now married a successful Professor and an influential leader in Tanzania. My cousin was my inspiration – she still is. Not only has she inspired me in pursuing an education but sister Grace has been an inspiration in her marriage. She made me see that it is possible to have a good marriage. She was the only figure in my life that provided evidence to a good marriage – that it is possible to have a faithful husband.

During my A levels, I decided to choose the same as my cousin sister. Okay, there were other factors involved too, I didn't like Physics and I didn't see myself becoming a doctor. But at the end of high school, I knew that I didn't want to be a nutritionist. So, I figured that I would pursue a Bachelor's Degree in Accounting and Finance (BAF) at Mzumbe University, one of the prestigious public universities in Tanzania.

In Jangwani Secondary School that's when I started to get involved in English activities such as debate competitions and school plays. I also represented my school several times along with other girls to the UN General Model Assembly that used to be held yearly in Karimjee Hall in Dar es Salaam, with attendance by representative from almost all secondary schools in the city. This increased my confidence and friends or contacts I made. These students I met most of them became successful in life some became fashion icons in the country, some wrote books – such as Constantine Magavilla the author of *'Life and You'*, who is also my role model; some became big businessmen or worked with international organizations etc.

Sometimes in our daily lives we stay inside our shells not wanting to come out, volunteering information, services or knowledge in fear of being seen presumptuous. You should always be respectable, but never be afraid to be bold and outgoing. When I was in high school someone mentioned that it's the same students that sometimes look a little presumptuous – *kimbelembele* in Kiswahili that make it in life. Do not be arrogant, of course, but we shouldn't make a point to hide in our shells. Come out and play! Hopefully, in doing so, you will in turn give permission to others to be their best as well.

SEXUAL CORRUPTION

Starting a new life away from home was a new experience for me. I had to move to Morogoro, about 200 kilometers away from Dar es Salaam; a three hours ' drive by car. I didn't have any background in Accounting, and here I was, enrolled in Accounting and Finance as an undergraduate scholar. You can imagine what a rough time I had with that subject. Our Accounting lecturer, Mr. Komunte a very good teacher I should add didn't help at all. He was very intimidating. He would often remind us that some of us would not make it to the finish line. Well, I did fail once during my study at the university, on the same subject. I had to retake the exam and luckily, I passed.

To be honest, I am not sure if I passed that exam on my own or if I was "enabled". It happened that during that exam, I was so shaky that I couldn't remember everything. As you might know, one wrong number in Accounting affects the whole table of answers. Prior to that, our lecturer had given a number of possible questions. So before the day of the exam, I wrote the answers down in a piece of paper in an attempt to cheat. The exams were often conducted in a big hall or at the Cafeteria hall where more than 200 students of different majors were accommodated at once. Unfortunately, one of the invigilators a young teacher saw me as I was copying the answers. He was a tutorial assistant at the time. He was handsome, and brainy. Although he was kind of arrogant, he was really nice. I thought he was appealing, although I had never thought of having a relationship with him.

The university was very strict about cheating. We would often hear about students being discontinued from completing their year of study because of this. And we heard that teachers would be given monetary reward if they caught a student cheating and had proof. That's why I knew that this was going to be the day I was sent home. As he walked towards my desk, I knew that he saw me. To my surprise, he came over quietly, pushed over the answering paper that was covering my '*migi*' (a slang word we used at University for 'cheating notes'), smiled, and shook his head as if to tell me to take it away, which I did. He did it so calmly that even those around me didn't notice what had happened. But I was too shaken and whatever was in my head was all gone I couldn't answer anything. So I failed that exam.

After that incident, I was so thankful to God and promised that I wouldn't use '*migi*' again. But that was not the end of it. A few days later, I met the young tutorial assistant at the library where I was reading. He came over to my desk; he greeted me and took my number. I think I was both shaken and experiencing butterflies in my stomach. I saw a few heads turn when he came over to talk to me. It was not normal for a teacher and a student to have a casual conversation like that. We started texting and being friendly from that time on. After all, he had saved my life. But it seemed he wanted to develop something more than just friendship. I could tell that he liked me from how he smiled at me, maintained eye contact and gave me more attention. However, I would just shrug it off every time I thought our conversation would lead to *that* direction. When the results came out and I had failed the exam, I knew this was trouble. And at the time, the tutorial assistant was coming onto me stronger than before.

I always wanted to stay away from the lecturers. I never thought that this would happen to me. My friends and I would hear stories around campus about lecturers getting involved with students so they would pass. Sometimes, we heard that some students flunked a class for over a year. It was also common to see a whole class graduating, yet one female student remaining behind to clear a subject that she had failed. It was usually the case of a relationship gone wrong or refusal to sleep with the lecturer.

I would go numb whenever I saw his messages or calls. He said that he would help me pass and now he was in control. I remember how he said it, "Don't worry, I will take care of it if you fail." I was scared that if I turned him down, that would make him upset with me. That would mean more problems for me. Then one day, he scheduled a date outside school in town. I knew what he wanted. He already was texting me, saying that he was thinking about me. That was one of the most difficult times for me as a University student. I liked him as a person and maybe I was a little infatuated with him but I wasn't ready to have sex with him. I mean, I felt like this was a bribe – and it was. I knew that if I refused, I would definitely flunk this subject. Okay, maybe it wasn't a definite fact, but he could make things very hard for me.

Eventually, I agreed to meet him privately. I remember how distraught I was before going out on the 'date'. I was in my dorm room, looking into thin air outside the window, praying to God, "No one can save me now but only You." I hadn't told anyone about this. Actually, this book is the first time that I reveal this incident. When we were in a private room kissing, I excused myself to the bathroom. It was torturous. I wasn't present in that room. In a way, I was in denial of what was happening – mostly quiet and replying only when necessary. I was deep in my own head and I had a terrible stomach ache. I was too nervous.

In the restroom, something happened that changed the course of events. I found out that I had started my periods. I don't think I have ever been so grateful to see my monthly flow like that moment. You can imagine how relieved I was. I believe God saved me that day. I know that if we slept together, I would have felt miserable, and he would have stolen my confidence and dignity. But the truth is, even though we didn't sleep together, it still troubled my mind. The fact that I went to meet him in private, the fact I was thinking of having sex with him – thinking that I had no way out – it haunted me to think how weak I was. I couldn't get over it. Why didn't I just say no and face the consequences? He didn't steal my dignity, but I was left feeling less of myself. Especially since I still had to communicate with him – asking about the results of the exam that I had to re- sit. I'm glad I managed to get out of situations where we would be in private together again. I would just give excuses not to.

I always wondered what he thought. Did he think that I had wanted to have sex with him willingly or did he know that I didn't want to yet he pushed me anyways, thinking that he had a stronger hand? Sometime later, I would see this lecturer in the university hall when I enrolled for a Master's Degree. Across the hall, we would look at each other, no smiles, just a stare for a few more seconds than we should have. Then we would both turn away. It wasn't a look friends would give each other. I could see that we both felt cheated or taken advantage of. Him for giving a favour that I never returned and me, being forced to have physical contact in circumstances that I otherwise wouldn't have.

This whole ordeal made me think about women who had it worse than me. How devastating and disturbing it might be, not to have anyone to share it with – to keep a secret for the rest of your life. There are women who walk feeling undignified. Some think that they deserved it, to be 'raped' in this way.

Post Undergraduate Graduation

A few months after I graduated from Mzumbe University, Ms. Mentor[5] took me back to work for her Public Relations company. I had previously worked for her after High School as her personal assistant. After university, my task was to assist with the accounts and run other errands while I waited for my 'big job' as a fresh graduate. This sounded great, I could earn a few shillings and at least I wouldn't be idle at home.

Working for Ms. Mentor was the best thing that ever happened to me as a young woman. Although I already had two part time jobs before meeting her (one as a day-care teacher and another as a presenter at a famous radio station in the city), she is the one who motivated me to own a business. Through her, I saw the importance of the mentor - mentee relationship to guide an individual to see the window of possibility to their desired future. When we first met, Ms. Mentor had just graduated from university in Europe. She showed me how people differ in mentality. Most people would look for a job on completing their degree. I remember asking myself in that small two-roomed office, *'Do you think Ms. Mentor's children would be*

---

[5] Real name has been concealed

motivated to go and work for someone or build their own businesses?

I was Ms. Mentor's first assistant. She didn't have an office when I started working for her. She would operate from her home and sometimes from her car. I saw how she established the company with just a handful of clients. She put her best into the business to deliver the best to her clients. Coming back as a graduate from university and dealing with her company's financials – which entailed depositing the cheques she would get from her jobs – and seeing how well she was doing, opened my eyes into this new world where owning and being your own boss was possible.

Ms. Mentor came from a well to do family. Her father is one of the influential former politicians in the country. We once passed by her parents' home in Masaki – one of those posh neighbourhoods where the rich, influential and expatriates live in my city. I was impressed by what I saw; their house was a work of art. This was at a time when our family had relocated from Upanga, a decent neighbourhood near the city centre to Tabata, which was a lower class area. My dad couldn't afford to buy the flat we lived in since the company that he was working for was selling their apartments. They stopped providing housing for their employees. Unlike Upanga, Tabata didn't have tarmac roads in between streets; houses were crowded and the majority of people living in our new street were poor.

When we moved to our new house, I hated the neighbourhood. I remember how at night, I would dream of Upanga – when I had dreams at night the settings of events would still be in the streets of Upanga. We had lived in Upanga for almost 20 years. You can imagine my feelings when we visited Ms. Mentor's wealthy looking residence. She offered me some snacks and a drink. I wasn't comfortable to use a fork and a knife at that time – a fresh university graduate. I still had a lot to learn. I learnt a lot of things while working with Ms. Mentor. Among them was how reading books would help motivate my ambitions and make me a better individual. These books were in the office's book shelves and I read them during my lunch break or when I had some free time.

A conversation I had with another assistant that was there the second time I worked with Ms. Mentor, played a major role in pushing me to be a business owner. She was also a university graduate. According to her, Ms. Mentor had said that she is the kind of a person that could own her own business, unlike me. I don't clearly remember everything that we spoke but it seemed like Ms. Mentor thought that I did not have what it takes. I considered this to be untrue because there was no relevance of these comments to achieving better performance unless they were directly told to me. This made me ask myself a lot of questions. Why would it seem like I wasn't capable of owning a business?

This didn't discourage me. I really didn't care and I held no grudge. It just opened my eyes a little more that there are people who can and those who can't own a business. I knew for sure that I wasn't going to be one of those who can't, and settle to being employed for the rest of their lives.

AMBITION RETARDATION

Many things can retard a person's ambitions in life. Becoming a business owner, going out for your dreams and not conforming to the status quo has a lot to deal with self-esteem. Where do you get that? Maybe from your family, friends or a mentor supporting you financially or building you mentally, assuring you that you can do it and you deserve the best.

Where we live – whether in a rich suburb or a slum –

affects our self-esteem and how we see ourselves. Most of the time you can tell, just by looking at someone if they are from a well-off family or they are struggling – you just can't lie for long – maybe that's why it was concluded that I couldn't own a business. The new house was unfinished when we moved in. There was no ceiling board in the bedrooms only in the living rooms, we could directly see the *mabati* – steel roofing. Sometimes, I would just lie on my bed and stare up at the roof. The toilet in the house wasn't finished, so we used a pit latrine outside the house. You can imagine the psychological torture that we went through as a family, coming from a house that had a bathtub before this. I couldn't invite my friends over. The walk from the main road to our house was torture to go through. If you use the shortcut on foot, you would cut across people's shabby houses and yards. If you passed by in a car, then you would see the damaged muddy road – especially when it rains.

Moving around in Upanga was easy. Taking a taxi wouldn't cost much. But in our new neighbourhood in Tabata, which was far from the city centre, you couldn't afford to take a taxi, at least not as a fresh graduate. To make matters worse, Tabata was also famous for public transportation hurdles– typical case of a big population and few buses. In Upanga, my siblings and I had a lot of friends. But I hardly invited anyone to our new home, unless it was necessary that they had to drop me home after a night out. I remember once when my friends and I went to the beach, one of my best friend's brother had a car. Being a responsible brother that he was, he said he must return each of his sister's friends home. When we reached at my house, my friends wanted to go to the toilet. I remember apologizing to them for the condition of our toilet. I guess to them it was odd but maybe not to the extent of my shame.

Another deadly agent that retards people's minds is drugs. If any of my classmates from primary or secondary school heard that I would smoke weed later in life, they wouldn't agree. I wouldn't agree either. But that is what happened. This was just after I had finished High School. That is when a friend introduced me to a whole new world.

I just wanted to remain a casual smoker. I smoked only in front of this friend of mine, or sometimes at home when nobody was around. Nobody else saw me smoking – I would do this indoors. It just wasn't expected of me to behave that way. My friends, siblings and relatives had this image of me which I wanted to maintain. I was very careful about it. I wanted to keep it as contained as possible. I didn't smoke daily and could go for weeks without it. I never smoked a whole blunt at a go; I knew that would knock me out. I only took three or four puffs each time I smoked. I didn't think of myself as a smoker per se. But that's not how drugs work. They lure you slowly and before you know it, you are hooked.

I would take a blunt or two from my friend and keep it for later use in my house. I never used to buy it myself. But, I remember once, I had nothing on me and my friend was unreachable. I had to buy it. Until today my friend who introduced me to weed never knew that I had ever bought it by myself. This friend was regretful to have influenced me in that direction – I thought that was enough guilt on my friend I didn't want to add on it - so I never mentioned it.

The time I went to buy weed for myself was on holidays at home in Tabata. We had a break of few months from undergraduate studies in Morogoro. This was probably during my second year of study. I approached a vendor who sold second hand clothes, famously known as *'Mitumba'* in Kiswahili. And he agreed to introduce me to a dealer in our neighbourhood. The dealer lived in a shabby small house. When we got to the house, the Mitumba vendor called for someone to come out and he left me there. So many thoughts went through my mind. I was so nervous through the whole experience that even today I wouldn't be able to find my way back to that shabby house.

A few seconds later, a middle aged woman came out. If you saw this woman in a market you wouldn't know that she sells weed. She looked very normal, respectable, well-tempered and calm. She even looked like she didn't smoke it herself. I asked for the price and bought enough – about ten joints. So I didn't have to go back again and left. I remember after the holidays I took some back with me to the university and smoked when I was stressed and when my roommate wasn't around.

Now when I look back, I think that the details of this encounter were quite strange. The appearance the woman left me with two kinds of impressions. She managed to make me feel somehow relaxed – because she looked like she could be my aunt or big sister. So in a way this made buying weed feel like not a big deal. But on the other hand, she also ended up making me feel weird buying from such a figure. It was confusing. I guess I was expecting a big muscled-up druggie to come out of that door – like how they portray the drug dealers in the movies.

At that point, I really felt like a druggie after buying the weed myself. I also didn't like myself when I looked in mirror. I thought that my appearance changed. I thought I started to look like a junkie. I didn't want that.

I came to realize that many successful and influential people smoke weed. That felt strange to know. But then this behaviour starts out when most people are young, maybe in college. These are the same people that would later become the future CEOs and leaders in the country. I imagined some big decision made by people who are (on the low) druggies. It's crazy. This world is crazy.

It happened that one day, I started having my menstrual periods with heavy tissue discharge. This scared me. I went to the hospital thinking that there was something very wrong with me. Thank God, my father had health insurance that covered the whole family. I could just see a doctor without notifying anyone. Before I went to see the doctor, I promised God that if He let me be safe I would never smoke weed again. The doctor told me that I had a miscarriage. And that's how I stopped smoking. I thank God, because of His protection and grace that weed smoking didn't turn out to be a lifelong addiction.

2. WHY CHINA? SAYING GOODBYE

The heart of man plans his way, but the Lord establishes his steps.

Proverbs 16:9 | ESV

Corporate World

In the developing world, most graduates dream of employment. There isn't a system in place to support business startups. If there is any, then they aren't very popular. And that should tell you something about the system. Like most graduates, formal employment was the only option for me until I started reading books and became exposed to the idea that it's possible to own a business and have passive income. I got my first job as an accountant – a reconciliation associate – at one of the biggest cigarette companies in the country. However, I quickly got bored within the first eight months. I then moved to the Internal Audit department. But before I moved, a famous bank in the country, called me for an interview. They had a graduate management trainee position where you would receive training in South Africa in their sister company for about a year before you got placed in a management position.

After I went through all the interviews and signed so many legal documents such for new employees, the Bank decided to go with only one candidate for the job that graduated from the UK. I remember two of us – the girl who graduated from UK and I meeting with the Managing

Director for the Bank. After a short introduction the meeting was finished. I think this was when they decided to go with the other girl.

I almost quit my job at the Cigarette Company because I was led to believe by the HR of the Bank that the position was mine – after signing all the documents and also because they were telling to resign and prepare for the new position. I sought legal advice from a law firm in Dar which represented me in getting compensation from the company. Instead, the Bank offered me another position, so that I would drop the claims. I was told that I was still young and all HR personnel talk among themselves. This wouldn't be good for me, they said. I later found out that the bank's HR had similar 'mishandlings' with other people in the past. I wasn't the first to be mistreated this way.

After a number of arbitration hearings, I stopped going. I thought of how my mother used to go to court to seek compensation on behalf of our grandmother who had a train accident years ago before we were born. My mom made follow ups for years and didn't get compensated. I didn't want to waste my time on this. I knew that this position was not the only way for me to succeed in life. But I was glad that I had taught them a lesson. They couldn't just mistreat people like that. I mean, they actually employed a lawyer who showed up to each hearing. I thought that was enough.

So I continued with my work at the Cigarette Company and moved to internal auditor department. This was more challenging and interesting to me. First, I got an opportunity to know functions of different departments in the organization by working with them. Secondly, there was a lot of travelling to branch offices located all over the country. The only problem was that auditors are nobody's friend. Our manager used to always say, "You need to develop a thick skin in this profession." When he would say this, I remembered how Ms. Mentor would say, "We are in a happy business Shubi, smile!"

I worked for three years as an internal auditor. During this time I started to become more interested in self-help books. 'Rich Dad Poor Dad by Robert Kiyosaki' was one of the books that I started reading. I learnt of the most important question – How long can you live, maintaining the same life style without a job? – I learnt about passive income and the true definition of financial freedom.

The book that provoked me to action was 'Think and Grow Rich' by Napoleon Hill:

"I bargained with life for a penny, And life would pay no more, However, I begged at evening when I counted my scanty store. For life is a just an employer, he gives you what you ask, but once you have set the wages, why, you must bear the task. I worked for a menial's hire, only to learn, dismayed, that any wage I had asked of life, life would have willingly paid."

You ultimately get what you want in life. But you have to know what you want and work hard to achieve it. In 'The Secrets of the Millionaire Mind' by Harv Eker, I learnt of the root causes of success, mediocrity and financial failure and how to change your life for the better. I recommend these books to you as they opened and changed my mindset. They cultivated the desire to have my own business and eventually have a passive income. My colleagues and I were obsessed about doing business; we would frequently talk about businessmen and life outside employment. At some time when there were retrenchments in the organization, we saw how people were not prepared for life of owning a business. And that even though they were given retrenchment package, with no experience and less confidence in running a business, the chances of success were slim.

With this job, I also got to meet businessmen who earned millions and I learnt of many opportunities that would provide extra income in agriculture and other sectors. It is these talks with my colleagues, day in and day out that built the fire in me and the confidence to seriously consider moving to China for my master's degree and try out in the business world.

WHY CHINA?

It was while I was at the cigarette company that I made my first trip to China in 2009 to visit my best friend, Dr Natasha Choka – whom we met at Jangwani Secondary School. After the trip, I came back to Tanzania with some women shoes, handbags and clothes to sell – it was my first trade to compensate for my flight ticket and expenses for the travel. This gave me an insight on how money can be easily multiplied. I also learnt how most of the world goes to China to buy products and sell them in their respective countries. I became interested with China. That was when I decided that I would go to study there for my master's degree and do business at the same time, hence, multiplying my money.

I started applying for scholarships to China. Then I realized that it was not so easy to get one unless you performed extremely well or if you had a relationship with a big shot in the government. With a 3.4 GPA that I scored in my undergraduate degree and no connections that could get me ahead, my chances of getting a scholarship were zero. I tried to get a loan from a student's loan body in Tanzania with no success. I remember leaving the loan board offices after they had turned me down feeling disappointed but being very calm. I decided that it would not go down in history that these institutions were the ones that stopped me from accomplishing my goals. I decided to set another goal, to earn a higher salary and save money to pay for my own education.

I knew that even if the cigarette company added the annual increment after the salary appraisal, the money would still not be enough to support my education in China. The salary you negotiate while being recruited would seldom drastically change yearly. And since it was my first job as a 'fresh from school' employee, my salary wasn't much. But I would often recall the words of my friend from the radio station, Gerald Hando who always believed in me more than I did in myself. He would tell me, "Shubi never settle for peanut money."

Meanwhile at the office, we were required to advance in higher education, by either getting professional accounting certifications such as a CPA and ACCA or a master's degree. That wasn't the direction that I wanted to take. I didn't want to specialize in accountancy. I wanted to get an MBA and start a business. Eventually, I enrolled for a Master's degree in Marketing Management at Mzumbe University in their Dar campus as an evening student. The company paid half of my tuition fee, so that was okay. I thought, it didn't hurt to get two masters degrees. I would first get this degree, get a better pay because of it and eventually manage to pay for my MBA in China. Plus, I loved marketing. Pursuing this course would increase my skills for my future businesses.

But the job hunt didn't stop. The goal was to get a job with a better pay. I consistently followed up on friends working with recruitment agencies until it paid off. I got an offer from one of the leading banks in the country as an Analytic and Performance Manager for retail banking. I would have preferred to give a month notice but the vacancy had to be filled immediately. I gave a few weeks' notice and moved to my new job. This was in early 2011.

The feeling was amazing. I had a managerial position and a higher pay, which was what I wanted. I could finally see my dream – going to China and owning a business – coming to reality. But, the workload was as great as the pay. Being new at this position meant that I needed to spend more hours to learn of all the reports that had to be prepared and shared with the management; some were daily, weekly and monthly. Most of the time, I even worked on Sundays till midnight. I would drive to church and head to work after.

Just after I moved to the bank, we started our final exams. It was some time in June of 2011. It was exams; finish my dissertation and graduate – in that order. Although it was very stressful, I felt very confident in myself. I just got a new job in a bank with a better pay, which meant I got to work with young brilliant minds and highly professional people. Nearly everyone drove a fancy car. My boss – the head of Analytic and Assets department drove a classy power engine BMW sedan while others drove Mercedes Benz and other expensive cars.

I on the other hand, drove my dad's old Toyota Mark II. But I had no complaints. In fact, I loved it. I started driving when I started working at the bank. Actually, I didn't even have the time to go to driving school. My brother Ibrahim is the one who would drive my sister Siima and I. Now that he was going back university to another city, I had to learn. In the evening, Ibrahim would give me driving lessons at a football field near our house. I was on the road in less than a week. I loved driving. I was overtaking and generous on speed within a month.

Everything in my life gave me this adrenaline rush. I felt like a shark. I became arrogant and I believed in my own ability to do things. I guess I felt invincible and that's why I used migi, again. A few people I knew were also using migi in the final exams. It was no big deal. Perhaps I was less careful and maybe fate wasn't on my side. I was caught, again. This time, I was disqualified from my studies. Perhaps I needed to learn a lesson about cheating. It seems like I didn't learn my lesson from my bachelor's years. Some of my classmates consoled me. They would ask me, "But why did you use 'migi'. We know these things aren't difficult for you." I think that, this time it wasn't like I needed migi. I used it because I thought I could get away with it.

I remember that evening after a meeting with the Dean and other teachers, I got in my car with a friend who used to ride with me back home, the windows were up, and the tears came down. I cried. No, I wailed, loudly while my friend remained quiet. She just listened. Then I wiped my tears and started driving. I felt a certain relief. Driving can be therapeutic, a kind of sport that makes me relax. Especially late at night and there are few cars on the road.

The truth is, I was more upset about how this would appear on my records than the fact that I had been discontinued. I mean, I knew I was capable and better than that. But records will always remain. When I wiped my tears it was the last time I cried about this. I didn't want to talk about it with my family when I got home. I had no choice but to compose myself and be strong.

Only a few people knew about this. Even my siblings and some of my close friends didn't know. However, the dead of my department at the bank heard about this. He was also doing a master's degree in the same University. He told me that he knew what happened and that he was concerned that maybe I couldn't prepare well for my exam because of too much work. It is possible that this contributed to it, but I felt that the incident had to happen. I wasn't very upset about it because I knew that I would be heading to China for my MBA in a few months. This incident made it easier for me to tell my boss about my plans to resign and go for further studies in China. He had become more than a boss to me, more of a friend. Before the incident I was troubled on how I would break the news. I knew how demanding the work was and how tedious it was to recruit and train another person for the position till they became competent.

INCUBATED IN CHINA

When I got disqualified, I was humbled. I learnt that being the best isn't as important as being honest and following the rules. For example, people are ready to work with someone who is humble and trainable, even if he is less talented. This reminds me of an intelligent but arrogant Manager who had poor people skills and relationships. He thought no one could touch him. The top management relied on him and sometimes they openly overlooked his weaknesses. He finally got fired over a sexual harassment scandal. Eventually, things catch up on you. You never get away free.

Later on in life I read the Bible and got to see how God hates the proud in any form whether because of beauty, or wealth. In the book of 2 Chronicles 26 we read about King Uzziah whom after his success he became proud which led to his downfall and finally death. Another is the story of King Hezekiah [2 Chronicles 29 – 32] who succeeded in all that he did and later became proud. But we see that King Hezekiah later repented and the Lord delivered him.

After reading this, now I always try to humble myself before God. For it is He, who provides us with everything. Being proud or arrogant only invites the wrath of God and fall from His grace. [Leviticus 26:19 NIV] I will break down your stubborn pride and make the sky above you like iron and the ground beneath you like bronze.

The Plan

When I was at the cigarette company, I saw how people who knew that employment wouldn't bring them financial freedom would stay at the same company sometimes for ten years or more. Since they had families that depended on them, they couldn't risk leaving to pursue a business. They needed stability and couldn't afford uncertainties that starting a business would bring. I thought to myself, if I wanted to start on a business venture, I needed to start early before I too get scared.

The plan was to do two years in China, pursuing my master's degree while trying to set up a business. I thought that even if I failed, I would have earned my degree. I would gladly be open to marriage afterwards and get back to employment knowing that I had tried and failed. It was the craziest thing I had ever decided to do. I couldn't tell many people of this idea. My boss at the bank didn't understand why I had to go to China. He tried to persuade me to stay. He said in a few years, I could be the head of the department in Retail Banking. He also said that being employed could help me get a mortgage. At the time, he had already got his mortgage and was building his dream mansion. I saw the blueprint of his house. It was superb.

It was tempting but I would tell myself that if I spent ten years being employed and ten years building a business, I would rather spend my years on the latter. It's better to build a business no matter how small but it is, it would still be mine. One day, I would hand this business to my children. However, even if I reached the highest rank of employment as a CEO of a company that wasn't mine, I could never hand this down. I thought that there is no security in being employed. I also didn't like it when someone put a ceiling on how much I could earn, using my brain in doing a few repeated duties in a company while I could do a lot more and diversify. My initial idea was to engage myself in a solar business. I didn't know how but I knew I would find a way.

I remember, after I resigned from the cigarette company, one of my bosses there joked that at least now it would be okay to have dinner with me – since I wouldn't be his subordinate anymore. And we did have dinner. We would meet up each week for dinner. We had no sexual relations. It was just dinner. We enjoyed each other's company, joked and laughed about everything. Dinner was on him, of course. I tried to pay once but I joked that he is still being paid more than I, so let me not try to be funny. It was hard to tell him when the time came to hand in my resignation at the bank and move to China. I esteemed his intelligence – he was probably one of the most intelligent and successful people I had chance to spend time with. So I thought he would think I am crazy to quit yet another job in pursue of a dream that was uncertain in China. Well, it wasn't so bad when I told him. He encouraged me. He thought that I would make it with the drive that I had. He also commented on the technical knowledge about the solar business and the language skills needed in China.

I remember praying before I left, "God please go with me to China." It was scary but I knew if He went with me, I would be okay. Everything would work out.

3. LUOSHI ROAD – EARLY CHALLENGES

No temptation has overtaken you except such as is common to man; but God is faithful, who will not allow you be tempted beyond what you are able, but with the temptation will also make the way of escape, that you may be able to bear it

1 Corinthians 10:13 |NKJV

THE POWER OF YOUR MIND

I have come to believe in the power of our thoughts in manifesting what we concentrate on just as explained in the documentary called 'The Secret' and in several books, 'Think and Grow Rich' by Napoleon Hill being one example out of many. When I was preparing myself to move to China, I had a budget on how much I would need for my travel ticket, school fees, living allowance and accommodation. But when the day had arrived for my departure, having bought the ticket already, I realised that I was short on money.

I was waiting on the Pensions Fund that had my savings to transfer the balance to my account. But that would have only been done by the time I got to China. I wasn't sure how much savings I had. To my surprise, they credited my account with the same amount that I had estimated when I made my budget. It was almost the same figure. I was really surprised and I remembered about the power of my thoughts and visualization.

After this experience, I became confident in this theory. Whenever I struggled with being paid low salary in China through teaching jobs in the university, as low as 800 RMB (about $120) per month, I aimed higher. I had a notebook with my prayer points on it. I would read them during my time of prayer. I would read Bible verses also to remind God of His promises. To tell you the truth, when I wrote in my notebook that, I was going to receive 10,000 RMB every month; that seemed like a big number. At the time, I would receive less than 10 percent of my 'visual' monthly. Sometimes, I would even shyly smile by myself, thinking of how embarrassing it would be if someone read my note book and saw that I was aiming that high from where I was.

I would read it out loud since I knew that the number doesn't really matter. It matters that you see it and that you put your faith in it while you work hard in what you do. And before you know it, doors will open to accommodate your belief. And it happened just like I claimed it. I started earning more than 10,000 RMB per month. This made me even more astonished of how true it is that 'thoughts become things.' You can also read more on visualization from Napoleon Hill's 'Think and Grow Rich'.

Most of the time, we don't have because we don't ask or we don't know how to ask – asking for the wrong reasons. [James 4:2-3 NLT] *You want what you don't have, so you scheme and kill to get it. You are jealous of what others have, but you can't get it, so you fight and wage war to take it away from them. Yet you don't have what you want because you don't ask God for it. And even when you ask, you don't get it because your motives are all wrong—you want only what will give you pleasure.* And many times we ask but we don't believe with certainty that we deserve what we ask for. This was one of my reminders to God every time I read out my requests to him from my note book. [Mark 11:24 NIV] *Therefore I tell you, whatever you ask for in prayer, believe that you have received it, and it will be yours.*

Your mind doesn't care what you feed it, it will produce results. I also found that to be true when I passionately said, "I am going to hurt you" – I will dwell more on this in the 'Path to Love' chapter ahead. If you intend to do good, opportunities will open up for you to do so. If you plan to do evil, demons will gladly assist to its manifestation as well. You need to be careful on the things you get fixated on. [Hebrews 12:2] The kind of music you listen to, the books you read, what appears on your social media page and so on. All these feed your mind. You also need to be careful on what you say to others. And most importantly, what you say to yourself. So now, I have set a new number to achieve and positive visualizations and prayers for myself and my loved ones. Your faith is real.

Racial Challenges

I was broke within a year in Wuhan. I had no income and no business. Life was also a little bit more expensive than when I had visited in 2009. Initially, I thought I would find partnerships in solar business and real estate. I found out that it was not as easy as I thought. First of all, the Chinese wouldn't partner with anyone unless you had 'guanxi' – strong relationships. This was especially true for big businesses. I had approached one businessman's son who also worked with the district government in Wuhan and gave him my proposal on the demand and the business mapping of real estate in Tanzania. His response made me realize that Chinese businessmen are more comfortable in China; and if they are to move and venture abroad, it had to be a big project, preferably that involved the government.

My former boss was right about the technicalities of starting a solar business. The idea seemed less interesting to me after I made more research and found out that most customers would be located in the countryside, with less purchasing power. I also learnt on the existence of bigger companies and projects that had extensive distribution channels that would even supply the solar panels to communities on credit. My original ideas couldn't work, at least not right away. And now that I was running out of money, I needed another plan fast.

I started applying for temporary English teaching jobs. This was the only job that I could do in my city, considering that I was holding a student visa with no Chinese language skills. I sent about twenty copies of my resume to different kindergartens and middle schools. I had to remove some of the experience from my CV and emphasize on the day care job I had after completing my O level education. I mean, who cares if you have accounting and analytic skills when they need you to play and sing with students?

When none of them replied to my emails, I started calling these schools and recruitment agencies. Most of them were quite impressed and I got invited for an interview by most of them. When I arrived at the interviews, I realized that they didn't expect me to be black or African. My classmate from Russia who arrived in Wuhan at the same time that I did, got a teaching job way too easier. He had started learning English when he arrived in Wuhan, so his English wasn't very good at the time. I came to learn that English teaching jobs preferred a white person regardless of where they are coming from.

Sometimes they didn't even have to be qualified. They just had to be white.

I was called to more than 20 interviews. Finally, one woman agreed to hire me only if I said that I was from Brazil. This was my first teaching job. She said that her customers wouldn't accept being taught by an African. I was so uncomfortable with this. I was assigned to tutor a VIP client. But we only met twice, they – they were a couple dropped out of class. I guessed they felt that they were being taken for a ride. Since my discomfort showed and I couldn't answer when they asked about culture and details about my "origin".

At the same time, my new boss informed me that another client didn't want to take my class because I am poor. They said I came from a poor country and I looked poor. I knew that I didn't look shabby and I had some decent clothes. Well, maybe, not expensive ones. Then I thought of how most white people dressed really casual especially as an English teacher in Wuhan. I was convinced that this was about the color of my skin and what they thought it represents.

Little did they know, most of the African students that get scholarships to China, are sons and daughters of high government officials, well respected in their countries and definitely not poor. I hadn't bought enough 'decent' casual clothes considering my tight budget. My boss, who knew that I wanted to do business in China, advised me on taking care of my appearance first. She said that Chinese people care about appearance. What brand is your watch? Shoes? Clothes? Handbag? Cellphone? and so on. Well, you should learn this, how you present yourself is vital to your success. This is not just in China.

This experience was an eye opener for me about discrimination of skin color and financial status, or should I say, among people who look wealthy or well off. There are strong debates on racism amongst the African community in China. In reality there is racism and discrimination everywhere in the world. There are different types of discrimination that involve skin color, gender, financial position and so on. Some are more eminent in different countries or community groups than others.

It is astonishing how black people who complain about discrimination on skin color can also discriminate their own people, giving more value to the ones who are lighter in skin tone. This has led to most of the black skinned women to feel the need to bleach their skin to feel more beautiful or attractive.

When I found out that even the Chinese women some of them lighten their skin to be whiter, I was convinced that this is the disease of the mind. We have been brainwashed to believe that light skin is better than darker skin tone. Imagine this, African women who bleach their skin would love to have the yellow Chinese complexion but some of the Chinese women think that their complexion isn't attractive unless it is whiter. I strongly believe that we should love our own skin, that which we were born with.

Self-love and positive outlook on oneself is very important. There are always going to be voices telling you "you are no better" – unjust treatments. But the voice within you has to be stronger than these voices outside. That's when you win and their voices will not bother you. Although the racism I encountered in China was not severe, it really didn't bothered me.

You can receive unfair treatment from people of your own continent, country, city, family and even people you consider friends. You shouldn't give anybody the power to validate your worthiness or belittle you. [*Titus 2: 14-15 | AMP*]

"*Who gave Himself on our behalf that He might redeem us (purchase our freedom) from all iniquity and purify for Himself a people [to be peculiarly His own, people who are] eager and enthusiastic about [living a life that is good and filled with] beneficial deeds. Tell [them all] these things. Urge (advise, encourage, warn) and rebuke with full authority. Let no one despise or disregard or think little of you (conduct yourself and your teaching so as to command respect)."*

Everybody is entitled to their opinion; your focus shouldn't be to change people's minds. What you should focus on is how you see yourself. You should know your own worth. And then focus on your journey to greatness that you wouldn't stop to throw stones at everyone who thought of you unworthy. Always remember to be so good that they can't ignore you. And if some doors won't open because of discrimination then build your own doors and never give up. There are always people who will be willing to cooperate with you.

FROM A CORPORATE EXEC TO INSTALLING HAIR EXTENSIONS

My account was almost close to zero before I got my first teaching job. I remember asking myself, "*So Shubi, what can you do? What can you offer to get some money?*" Well, I knew how to install human hair extensions. I was doing it on myself since I arrived in Wuhan. I couldn't go to someone to do my hair since I didn't have much money. And I knew I would get frustrated if I paid someone only for them to do it badly. So it was either I did hair or starve. It was *that* bad.

I prepared an ad with the last money that I had and placed one at the notice board in my dorm and others in a neighboring university. But it rained on the next day and the posters were washed away. I had to email students to spread the word around from the contact list I had – since I was the communication leader for the foreign student's union body. Although I charged lesser than the market price, I got a few clients. I was very slow compared to others who had more experience in installing hair extensions. But I still managed to get five regular customers who kept me afloat. I would charge 70 RMB while other hair makers charged about 100 RMB. I would get 350 RMB a month, on average. But it didn't feel so much since I would spend whatever I got right away.

It is during this time that my trust in God increased. It often happened that I would have my last meal in the fridge and no money at all. Then out of nowhere, someone would call and say they wanted to do their hair. This happened a couple of times to the point that even when I would have no money and not knowing where my next meal would come from, I would still be calm and peaceful. Someone would just call and ask if I had time to do hair.

Before I came to China, I had a friend who had been in a similar situation. She would wake up with no money and no food in the house. Yet it would often happen that someone that owed her money (that she has long forgotten about), would call her to give her money back. When she explained this to me, I didn't quite relate to her or understand them. When it happened to me, then I remembered about her story.

Once I remember there was this girl who came to install a weaving, she came with her friend. They were very loud and would speak in their vernacular language. I'm sure that my next door neighbor had trouble concentrating in her room because of how loud these customers were. As an introvert, I like to stay in my own head, unless I have to come out and entertain someone. On that day, I felt the pain of selling my time to people that I would otherwise not spend time with.

When I told my dad that I was making hair to survive, he got so emotional that I could hear his voice breaking over the phone. But I told him to be happy and proud that I am fighting.

In those days, I often recalled how I had made it to the 'big leagues'. I mean, I had made it as a manager in a one of the top banks in the country, sitting with the big boys discussing the performance of the retail banking and receiving a decent pay. *"Look at where your stubbornness has gotten you,"* – sometimes I would tell myself and laugh at myself. These thoughts would pop up when I was in difficulties. I often had to tell myself, *"I know you – you better buckle up and shut up because we are doing this"*. I knew this was just part of the journey.

Before I started making hair, I contemplated with myself and got myself to ask my former boss at the cigarette company for help (the one who asked me out for dinner). We were friends, so I knew that he would respond with kindness. When he would travel for work – after we had started having dinners, he often came back with gifts for me – from watches, lipsticks to shoes. He was rich, I knew this. But when I asked for help he didn't help. We lost contact after that. He contacted me after sometime and he asked me what was wrong, why weren't we chatting anymore. I asked him why he didn't he help me. I knew he could.

"I don't know," he said.

I knew what he meant. That was the kind of answer that I usually give when I don't want to explain further. Anyway, I felt like I didn't really matter to him. It felt like I was a break he took from his busy schedule to have a laugh. We never had a serious conversation. It was always a laugh about this or a joke about that. I was good company, that's it – charming, young, beautiful and ambitious. I often wondered that maybe all the chatting, gifts and dinners were to woo me until when he could press for more than just friendship. Since we were far from each other now, that didn't seem feasible. Hence, maybe that's why he had no motivation to help. Later on, I came to appreciate the fact that he didn't help me. It actually built me. If he had helped me, I would later feel belittled in some way. I have learnt to never accept or ask for a handout – perhaps a loan but not a handout. You don't want to lose your self-respect as you're building your empire. Did he know this? I don't know. But all in all, I thanked him for not helping me out – for not giving me a handout.

When They Give You a Chance!

I finally got the chance to teach oral English at my university. The job required me to be in class every morning from 7 – 7:30 am, revising new words with students and help them speak English. It also required me to have longer evening classes each day of the week except Saturday. The pay was too little compared to the amount of work we did, we had to make the students be interested in learning and encourage them to interacting in class. At the time, the pay was 800 RMB (about $122) per month which was hardly enough. But I managed to start buying fashionable jewelry – earrings and necklaces – and selling them in Tanzania. I started making money. And later, I started selling human hair extensions, which was better since I would get a higher profit with less effort. The amount of profit I would get by selling hair extensions to ten people – each head would need a minimum of three pieces of hair extensions – was equivalent to the profit made selling 200 jewelry pieces.

I also tutored a few students privately. They were preparing for the IELTS exam conducted by the British Council. Although the pay was very little as well, life was better for me. I was even able to buy a ticket, travel back home and contribute to my younger sister's wedding in December 2013. I was happy to be able to do all that.

When they give you a chance, no matter how small, take it and make sure they never forget it. Make it bigger, kill it! – once again words of my friend from the radio station in Tanzania. If I remember correctly, he was suspended at some point. I don't remember the reasons for his suspension, but when he got back to work he run the morning show, analysing daily newspapers. This was meant to reduce his responsibilities, I guess. But he used the chance he was given and made it bigger. He gained fame with his sense of humor and having a fearless analytical point of view on the current affairs in the country. He became one of the most famous radio personalities who hosted a morning show in the country. He even got to brush shoulders with the President.

That's what I did with my part time job as an English tutor at the university. I would often did free classes when invited to do a presentation about my country and culture. You have to know that everything has to be built from somewhere. Don't be afraid to give more than you are paid for in the beginning. In the beginning it's not about money. This will give you the opportunity to network with more people and the more people you know the more doors will open.

But free classes should never mean less quality. In whatever field you are in, never underestimate these free or less paying jobs – a position that seems to be less than where you see yourself. This is your ladder and the rehearsal to more business and abundance if you perform well. Who knows, these 'small jobs' might turn out to be your niche.

I got more involved as a leader in my university through a Students' Union for foreigners. I started out as communication leader then later I became the vice secretary. I remember giving my time to help new students. I would pick them up from the airport or the train station at late hours. I also participated in organising events such as culture festivals.

The university leadership noticed my efforts in and outside the classroom. I was awarded a Friendship Scholarship in my second year of MBA. Only few people get this kind of scholarship in my university. My school fees and accommodation were covered. It was another breakthrough – one which I thank God and my university for. This was in my prayer list too. God answered me.

I later received a scholarship to pursue my PhD. And I got a job to teach International Marketing in the International Education department to undergraduate students at Wuhan University of Technology. They would study for three years in China and graduate in the USA, UK or Australia.

This teaching job didn't just come over night. I started out as an assistant, marking grammar in students' thesis and reports. Then I was given a chance to teach one topic as a tryout. When there was a job opportunity, my supervisor Zhang Xin Laoshi recommended me for the teaching position. The first semester was so surreal, having students sitting for your exam and submitting their work to you. Sometimes, I was like *"Wow, these guys trust me to manage this course all by myself"*! I cannot thank God enough for His grace upon my life in Wuhan.

I would remember how a few years back; I wasn't even qualified to stand in front of middle school pupils because of my skin color. But God opened doors to teach a business class in a university. God is awesome! I thank my teachers too for trusting me and giving me these opportunities. During summer, I would wear African print dresses while teaching International Marketing at the university. I felt like I represented my country and Africa.

However small the amount I got from doing hair or in part time teaching, I saved ten percent of the money as my tithe. When I got back home in Tanzania, I gave my tithe to my church. I wasn't going to church in Wuhan at the time. Actually, I didn't go to church for most of the two years that I spent taking my MBA - although I would fast and pray on my own. It wasn't until a friend introduced me to a church that I started going.

No Shame

No one should be ashamed of how they started out in life. The struggle you go through in life should motivate the youngsters. Nothing comes easy; it has to be built with time. It is possible that young people lack appropriate role models or mentors in their lives, that's why some think that fast money is a better choice. They turn to selling drugs or selling their bodies.

We need to hear more stories of successful people in our society on how they started out. How did they make it? It is encouraging to know that like ourselves, they too have passed some difficult times which are only temporary. If the right principles are applied, everyone can reach greatness. And definitely not by illegal or immoral conduct.

In Wuhan, I had met a Professor whom I thought might help me move ahead in my career by giving me a temporary job. Instead, he proposed that I become his mistress. He said that he was always thinking of ways to give me money. This happened at a time when my income was hand to mouth, uncertain of when the next income will be. I got very angry and I was taken back to the time when my tutor wanted to sleep with me as an undergrad student. This got me thinking that maybe it's my petite body and friendly self that makes people think they can take advantage of me.

Of course I didn't become his mistress and I ignored his calls. Around the same time, a friend of mine who was a DJ in Wuhan had told me about a job in the club. I would get paid handsomely in just a month. The work entailed dancing in the club in skimpy clothes. Through these experiences, I have concluded that if you don't have strong moral principles, it's so easy fall into immoral ventures to make money, especially as a woman. I remember looking in the mirror and asking *"Shubi who are you? Who mothered you? Who is your father? Who are you brought up to be? What is it that is expected from you, your siblings?"* I made a promise to myself that I would earn my money the right way.

Teaching International Marketing at Wuhan University of Technology

4. BETTER THAN YESTERDAY

Do the best you can until you know better. Then when you know better, do better

Maya Angelou

A Cussing Brainy?

I will never forget the question that David Kanume asked me. It still rings in my mind, "Shubi, why does a beautiful girl like you cuss?" Using the F word or sh** and other profanity was totally okay for me. I would use such language with my peers since my undergrad years. But I didn't use the word b*** – I thought it was too much and undermined women.

As mentioned before, I was the Vice President for the Students' Union called ICEA – International Cultural Exchange Association. David – a young Sierra Leonean man who is composed and disciplined. He was my superior in the Association and he made me question myself about how I used my tongue. Did I want to present myself as such a person?

"Shubi, why do you curse?" David would ask calmly. I felt quite shameful. This made me reflect on why I cussed so much. And why did people cuss at all? I realised that I felt that it made me look stronger. It was a way of putting my guard up, warning people not to mess with me. But after much thought, I could see that cussing makes someone look cheap; one who is not being able to defend her case like a civilized human being. Using foul language can be a defence mechanism.

There are schools of thought regarding this. While some people think that it's unladylike others think it's sexy for a woman, especially when used in the right place at the right time.

1 Peter 4:11 | NIV

If anyone speaks, they should do so as one who speaks the very words of God. If anyone serves, they should do so with the strength God provides, so that in all things God may be praised through Jesus Christ. To him be the glory and the power for ever and ever. Amen .

After meditating on this word on how God's children should speak, I was resolute to refrain from swearing as it surely doesn't glorify God. I would stop myself every time I would want to say a bad word because that's not how I wanted to present myself. I reflected and felt that wise and established people don't have to swear to make their presence known. In fact, it was very childish – only uncivilised people cuss.

Being close to God each day, humbling yourself before Him, reading His word, fasting and praying is very helpful since you can easily get back to your old conditioned self. You should remember that you always have an option.

Before giving a reply, take time to think about your answer. David never knew the effect he had on me. A few years later while we were in church I thanked him for his patience and his question.

Why do you swear?

We need people like these who would dare ask you questions like that. People who would be concerned enough to hold us accountable or inspire us to do and be better.

BEING SAD IS A SIN

I remember wetting my pillow with tears. One night, I said to myself and to God that one day when I am happy with the right man, I would cry tears of joy of how blessed I would be. And that has already started to happen in my life right now, with this amazing man that the Lord has blessed me with – my fiancé and soon to be my husband by His grace.

When I was too sad for a long time I later decided that being sad is a sin. We cannot be sad while waiting for God to answer. It will only prove of our unfaithfulness. So I found ways and activities to keep myself busy and happy. Every time my old self would want to plunge me into sadness, I would rebuke the devil, sometimes rebuking myself. We have to learn to totally wait on the Lord while just being happy, that way it makes God act faster.

A co-worker at the kindergarten said to me one day with a sad tone, as if envying me "Shubi, you, are happy." It was as if she had some restraints from being happy. This was the same time when I was going through some difficulties and pulling all strengths, holding onto my sanity. When she said this, I almost got pissed off on how she couldn't see that being happy is a decision that nobody can take away from you. I explained to her that not everything in my life was perfect but I chose to be happy everyday despite of that. I felt like I was too aggressive when I responded to her. She said she understood me. I wasn't sure if she really did – I hope she did and *I hope you do too*.

It helps to talk it out – just make sure you can trust the friends you confide in. During this time I had an Iranian best friend in Wuhan. She was an architectural student in the same university as I in Wuhan. Now, that I think about it, I think I might have tortured her with all my troubles – when lunch meeting turns to counselling and advising or just being my sound board. She made everything easier – to know that she was there to listen or just being by my side holding my hand. Other relief I got was from another very good friend, she is Chinese. She was not a student; she already graduated in the UK and now had a job in Wuhan. We got introduced and became friends right away. Whenever it got too much she would pick me up at my dorm and talk my head off over dinner. It is amazing how I connected with these two ladies beyond our cultural differences, we clicked. I will always be grateful for their presence.

I also learned that I was happier when I got up and did something instead of staying in bed. Don't wait to be invited to a party or an event. Make your own party. I noticed that when I had some activity to look forward to, I was happier. I interacted with more people and just relaxed and enjoyed life.

There are many things you could do. You could cook your favourite food and invite your friends to have some. You could take a walk in the park, enjoy the sunshine and nature. Ride a bike. Do sports. Go for window shopping – who cares if you don't have money to buy – you still can enjoy looking. Take yourself out for an ice cream. Just get out and do something. Do not be the kind of person who waits on other people to have fun. I used to be that kind of a person. Having a boyfriend was all the fun I knew. I waited on a boyfriend to arrange what we would do for fun. If I didn't have a boyfriend, I had less fun and less happy.

You should learn on how to have fun even when you are single. Plan interesting activities and just enjoy life. Sometimes, it was just a bunch of flower I bought for myself that brightened my little dorm room and my days. Remember it's a little happy here and there that makes a big happy! Being happy is a chain of events and moments. You can create them.

Do Better

There are many things that can disrupt your peace especially in this information age. Peace of mind is very important. People pursue it through different ways such as travelling to secluded locations, meditation, fasting, praying, and even engaging in sports. While others intentionally look for ways to be more peaceful, there are ways especially in our own lifestyles that can be a source of losing our peace.

INCUBATED IN CHINA

You are the most important relationship you have. You should not tolerate any other relationship that makes you lose your peace. I remember blocking one of my very good friend from my social media page because of the comments he would leave. I had told him that I didn't appreciate the comments but he didn't listen. So I blocked him. Not even our best friends or family should constantly make us lose our peace. Another example is a group of ex school mates that was posting porn in a group chat. It was disrupting my peace. After communicating with no changes, I exited the group.

You can birth awesome ideas that benefit you and your community if your mind is calm and peaceful. You need to constantly evaluate what is disruptive to your peace. You should also spend some time in nurturing that calm state of mind. Always try to do better. Reading to acquire knowledge is one way to it. If they say you are what you eat. Then you are definitely are what you read. Napoleon Hill in his life changing book 'Think and Grow Rich' says the way of success is the way of continuous pursuit of knowledge. This can mean reading self-help books or reading the word of God which brings more wisdom. [Proverbs 4:7]

My mother read the bible three times in her life from

the beginning to the end. This inspired me to start a journey of my own. I have now finished round one. Soon, I will start to read again, from the beginning to the end. This gives you more insight on who God is. And the more you know the word of God, the more confident you will be in your relationship with God and you will not be so easily shaken by tribulations.

How you present yourself is also very important. Most of the time people can conclude what kind of a person you are just by looking at your dress code. As you get better you also improve and become self-aware on what looks good on you and how you would like to represent yourself. Sometimes, it might seem like simple choices to make on what to wear, but it's not. Your choices send a message on how you think of yourself and ultimately how people will respond to you.

This is important to know – especially for women – because there are so many choices for us when it comes to the question of how we present ourselves, which dress to wear for which occasion. For most men the choices are limited unless if you are in a culture that's open to more styles. The choices for men could be, should I have a mohawk or a just a low cut. Should I dye my hair blonde, chestnut or just leave it black. Should I pierce my nose, wear earrings or no piercing? Tattoos or no tattoos? Should I wear striped jeans, slim fit jeans, baggy jeans – the choices are many.

Perhaps it's better to think from a point of view of how you want to represent yourself. Then it can be easier to decide on many things. They say don't judge a book by its cover. But the truth is, most of the time, when it comes to your appearance people make conclusions based on how you dress.

For women, the decisions are many – to apply lipstick or not, and if you apply, which shade of lipstick is appropriate. It happened that a leader in my church in Wuhan proposed that I should MC for an event. I asked myself – lipstick or no lipstick? Maybe no lipstick? Since you don't want the congregation to be fixated on my lips. If you are going to a corporate, official or wedding function. Maybe the choices wouldn't be the same. 14 inch, 10 inch, 8 or 2 inch heels? Cleavage or no cleavage? Long hair to your waist or short hair? How long should you let your nails grow out? How many piercing should you have? On your nose, tongue, eye brows? Let your conscience and the Holy Spirit lead you in such cases to decide. But, you should know, they all send a message.

5. STILLNESSS

The Lord is my shepherd; I shall not want.

He makes me lie down in green pastures.

He leads me beside still waters.

Psalms 23:1-2 | NKJV

FORGIVENESS

I made a vow of chastity in 2014 after I gave my life to Christ on March 2. I was going to wait until marriage to give myself to my husband. However, early on my journey, I was tempted and sinned. I was very sad and disappointed in myself for breaking my own promise to God. I prayed about it and asked God for forgiveness. But I felt like it was not enough. The guilt was unbearable. My conscience couldn't take it. I slept on the floor for five days, mourning, repenting in prayer. I also gave a peace offering to God. I wanted it to be difficult to fall into sin again and think that I could just make a simple prayer afterwards and get away with it. Of course, you should know that if you ask for forgiveness with a sincere heart, God forgives and you are set free. But I thought that if when we are happy we give a thanksgiving offering together with prayers, what about when we sin?

Do you take for granted God's graceful and merciful nature? Do you ask for forgiveness even before you commit a sin – knowing that God will forgive you anyways? These are important questions that we must ask ourselves to keep in check.

I thought of how much effort we make to reconcile

when we wrong people than when we wrong God. In the Bible, I saw how even when God forgives, you lose a certain amount of grace and privileges from Him. I remembered the story of Moses whom after his disobedience he didn't enter the promise land.

Then the Lord spoke to Moses and Aaron, "Because you did not believe Me, to hallow Me in the eyes of the children of Israel, therefore you shall not bring this assembly into the land which I have given them." [Numbers 20:12 | NKJV]

When I gave my life to Christ, I had the opportunity to listen to a series of teachings by a great man of God in my country. He was talking about breaking chains from ancestral sins or curses from worshiping other gods. He explained that sometimes you might be saved but you don't really experience breakthroughs in your life in finances, relationships and even spiritually. To break from these curses, something extra has to be done. My siblings and I gave 'the Gideon's sacrifice' (Judges 6), which imitates the way Gideon gave to break down strongholds of the other gods in our lives. This was an important sacrifice which was accompanied by a prayer of forgiveness and rebuking the devil's hold in any part of our lives.

I also gave a sacrifice to break any curse inherited from my name. I was given my aunt's name. Because when I analysed myself, I saw many resemblances with her character. She was very strict, I also am. Sometimes it's not always good, we are supposed to be gentle. *Let your gentleness be known to all men* [Philippians 4:5a NKJV]. She never married. At the age of 30, I still didn't like to commit to meaningful relationships. In fact, I run away from them. So I took no chances. I gave a sacrifice and broke devils' chains on whatever bad I might have inherited because of the name.

Through the writing of this book, I learned more of the grace of God through the blood of His son Jesus Christ. I came to understand that, there is no greater sacrifice we can give that tops the sacrifice of the blood of Jesus. He paid it all and if anyone is in Christ is a new creation. Only the blood of Jesus can take away our sins compared to before in the Old Testament where people gave sacrifice and burnt offerings. Ephesians 1:7 says that, "In Him we have redemption through His blood, the forgiveness of sins, according to the riches of His grace."

We should know that when we truly ask for forgiveness, we are forgiven and restored. But the devil, the accuser of men, will try to fill us with guilt of our sins and backsliding. We need to move on when we fall. The devil will try to convince you of the greatness of your sin. In turn, tell him of the greatness of Christ's righteousness. Just believe!

THIN LINE TO INSANITY

When I decided to break up with Zamani in Wuhan and wait on God for marriage (you will read more on this in the following chapter), it was difficult to withdraw from the relationship – mind you we didn't fight and I didn't hate him. This was in December 2013, just before I travelled to Dar for my young sister's wedding. I just made a decision to end it and I did. A few months after we broke up, he started dating again. I would bump into them around the dormitory.

It was more difficult when I returned to Wuhan in January. I had to deal with the emptiness of all the things we used to do together. Everything around me would remind me of the relationship. During this time, I felt like it was going through a double break up, one from him – in Wuhan and also from a man in Tanzania who had expressed his desire to marry me before I left for Wuhan.

It didn't work out for us. Seeing him at Siima's wedding celebrations was hard, but it also allowed closure. In few months, he was going to pay dowry for a girl he had met when I was away in Wuhan.

Although, I felt sad and lonely in the beginning I held on to God with everything I had. You have to know that when you want change, it's never going to be easy. At times, I thought I would go crazy because of the sadness I felt. My thoughts were confirmed when I learnt that a close friend of mine had to get treatment because of a mental disorder caused by life challenges. When I heard about this I continually gave thanks to God for keeping my sanity and holding me together through it all. It's not because I was strong enough but His grace.

The faces of my loved ones saved my life. I was so sad that I printed photos of my loved ones and I hang them on my bedroom wall. Whenever I felt lonely, I looked at all these faces and moments in my life. I got comforted that I had people in my life that loved me and this gave me a reason to smile and go on with my day.

When I was fighting to get out of this depression, I didn't even chew a gum. A chewing gum to me acts as a distraction. It gives me an escape. It keeps me charged up.

With the intensity of depression I felt, I thought I would become addicted to chewing gums. I didn't want to escape, I wanted to fight. I chose to refrain from alcohol for the same reasons. I didn't want to turn out an alcoholic as I tried to deal with my stress.

Not very long after, I experienced this beautiful stillness and peace. It's like I could slow down and hear myself breathing. I would come out of my dorm and notice the trees celebrating the day. Everything was so calm and beautiful. Fasting, reading and meditating on the word of God day and night was all the therapy I needed. I worshiped and pray at specific times throughout the day.

Self – Disciplining

All my life, I felt like I was missing something until I gave my life to Christ. Then I received peace, direction and contentment. The more I searched for closer fellowship with Him, the more content and peaceful I felt. The more I read His word, the more my perception of things in life changed. I slowly began shedding certain behaviours in my life.

INCUBATED IN CHINA

I used to love Hip Hop and R&B. I had a big collection of music. When I got saved, I kept on listening to these kinds of music. Then it happened that when I was praying one day, lyrics of a 'not so clean' song kept on popping up in my mind in the middle of the prayer. I pushed these thoughts away and continued with my prayer. This happened several times. And I decided that if I was seriously committed, I couldn't dance my head off to music that had sexual content in the daytime and worship God in the evening. [1 Corinthians 10:21-22] I believe it doesn't work like that. So I quit listening to these types of music and deleted all my collection. Music has the power to influence your emotions. Some music can make you feel a certain *type of way*, you know. This is worse if you are not married and abstaining from sex. I still like to listen and attend classical music concerts. I think this music is calming and there are no words that could pollute my mind.

I also decided that I wasn't going to go clubbing. I needed to find other ways to have fun. I felt out of place in the clubs. I didn't enjoy nor did I want to listen to the music being played there. I also didn't want it to be such an environment, where I could meet my future husband. I also didn't like the fact that young people would flirt with me. Actually, I felt like I was older than every man I met in Wuhan. But the real problem was where I met these kinds of men. I wanted something different. So I developed other hobbies and interests.

I tried yoga and meditation in pursuit of finding stillness and peace. I didn't spend time on these as they proved ineffective to me compared to fasting and finding quiet time with God. As a Christian fasting is a good way to lower yourself and communicate with God through His word, prayers, praise and worship. On days that I woke up craving for a sexual encounter, I would lower my body appetites by fasting, reading the word of God and worshiping. This worked for me. [Galatians 5:24 NKJV] *And those who are Christ's have crucified the flesh with its passions and desires.*

Sometimes, I also fasted from social media. I would stay out of Instagram or Wechat for weeks and use this time to read the Bible. I thought that if we could read the word of God as many times as we were on social media that would be pleasing to God and it would bring nourishment to ourselves. [Psalms 1:2-3 NKJV] *But his delight is in the law of the Lord, and in His law he meditates day and night. He shall be like a tree Planted by the rivers of water, that brings forth its fruit in its season, whose leaf also shall not wither; and whatever he does shall prosper.* I have noticed that when you are fasting, it's better not to visit social media pages. On social media, you are exposed to content that can disrupt your peace.

It came a time when I also gave up drinking. I was never a heavy drinker though. But I wanted to give myself to God without reservations. I hadn't been drinking for almost a year. Then I went to a networking event where they had a pint (very small amount) of wine in a glass for everyone, already set on the table. I drank this and later I started questioning myself whether I wanted to drink even just a sip. The next day was a Sunday, I went to ask my mentors whether it was wrong or not to drink even just small amount of wine. I told them after all even in the Bible Jesus turned water to wine for people to celebrate in some occasions. This is what they told me: "The devil has many schemes to get to you. If you can close doors and windows on temptations (drinking being one of them), it's better to do so."

Here are two examples of great men of God who sinned because of alcohol. In Genesis 19:30-38 Lot slept with his daughters. Another example from Genesis 9:20-25, Noah made and drank wine and his youngest son saw him naked and he called brothers as well. Because of Noah's drunkenness he uncovered himself and made his son sin.

As we were talking, I had an outer body experience and I saw myself defending my point so that I could get to drink, even if it was just a little. I sensed the Lord asking me, "Why are you defending this so hard? While you are talking about giving yourself to Me with no reservations, if I told you not to drink, would you refuse Me?" On my way back to my dorm that day I decided I didn't want to drink anymore.

Changing to becoming more like Jesus does not happen overnight. The more you seek a relationship with Him, the more you change. And you always have to recharge your connection with God every day in order to stay in line with what He wants – for you to be godly.

I remember before I met Deo (my fiancé) in Hong Kong, I was under a lot of pressure at work. I was also a bit nervous before meeting him. It was our first meeting since we started dating online. This was in April 2015. I started smoking cigarettes to calm my nerves – I had a lot of work to finish and pressing deadlines. This was an on and off habit that I picked in Wuhan. It started off by smoking one cigarette a night. Then, I quickly became a chain smoker. At this time I was an usher at the church I attended in Wuhan. When I fell off to this habit I stopped going to church for about two months, partly because I felt guilty. I remember opening up my luggage in Hong Kong and my clothes had this smell of cigarettes.

I used to smoke in my room in Wuhan or in the house while in Dar, when no one was around. Only two people saw me smoking cigarettes in my life. I had a reputation; I was an usher in church. I also didn't like making it a habit. It wasn't me and it wasn't expected of me. Deo thought the landlord was the one who smoked and he made comments about how he hated smoking. I'm glad I haven't smoked cigarettes since then. But you need to see how important we need to remain vigilant. [1 Cor 10:12 NKJV] *Therefore let him who thinks he stands take heed lest he fall.* It doesn't matter if you are an usher or a pastor. It doesn't also matter how long you have been standing with God. The devil is always there waiting. If there is an open window, he lets himself in.

6. PATH TO LOVE

Nothing feels better than when you love someone with your whole heart and soul and they love you back even more.

Karen Kostyla

Past Relationships

I had my first boyfriend in high school, in Dar es Salaam. We later broke up – I got suffocated with jealousy and trust issues. I was scared of how I could just leave someone in a minute, someone who had meant a lot to me – he was there for me during the passing of my mother.

After him I had a second boyfriend, whom after years of dating I also left him and started off a relationship with the third boyfriend (the third boyfriend is the one who will propose to getting married), literally the next a day. Well, for the second boyfriend at least I had reasons as he was unfaithful more than once.

But I later learnt that I was too quick to give up on relationships.

This made me scared of myself. Therefore, I ran away from men who approached me with seemingly real intentions for love. I avoided those types of men who seemed to love me and care and who seemed like we could have a chance of having true meaningful love. I was scared of hurting people and I knew what goes around comes around, after experiencing disappointments with my second relationship – leaving my first with no 'solid' reason. Instead, I dated men who seemed could take it even if I decide to leave. It was as if I was running away from true love. If a man really loved me I would see it as weakness I would be disgusted by it.

Before I came to China there was a young man (the third boyfriend above) interested to marry me. We had known each other for 10 years at the time. We had a relationship when he visited Tanzania. He was Tanzanian himself but lived with his family in a neighbouring country. He left after a few months. Although having a long distance relationship didn't work for us (we were both young and went on to date other people), we kept in touch. He was serious about marriage, that's what he said on several occasions. But I was doubtful. We didn't stay in the same city and he didn't have a proper job at the time.

I told him to move to Dar es Salaam and get a job, if he was serious. Just when I was about to travel to China, he moved to Dar and started looking for a job. We had discussed that the plan about marriage is still on, after I graduate. While in China I kept myself reserved for him and we kept on communicating. Sometimes, he would call and I would talk to his siblings and his mom. They were all excited for us and were looking forward for us to get together.

INCUBATED IN CHINA

At the time when I came to China, I had dreamt of building my own business. I had never stayed outside my country and I felt I needed to find myself. I knew I had to experience something (although I couldn't quite figure this out) but I felt I wasn't ready yet to stop and share my life with someone.

Sometimes, I think of how crazy it was for someone to tell me that they want to marry me, move to another country to get a job to make the relationship work, and me telling him to wait. Although, the move wasn't entirely because of me – his career development was more possible in Tanzania. That's why I advised him to consider the move, which I was right.

He said I ran away but I thought I wasn't ready. Thinking about it now, I feel like I was giving the relationship time to prove itself worthy, in a way. Although we had known each other for ten years, we lived apart for most of the time. We only had a relationship for three months while he visited Dar. I also felt that the beginning of a relationship is very important when it comes to marriage. We both had our faults. I couldn't get over the fact that when we met he lied about going to school in the UK – I have a big issue about people who lie, I wouldn't know how to trust you. For me, it doesn't matter if you are bad but just don't lie about it, pretending to be something you are not. Also, it bothered me that I was dating someone else (the second boyfriend above) when we met and that I jumped into a relationship with him, breaking off with the other person (the second boyfriend) in just a day.

The bottom line is, someone was asking for my hand in marriage but my dreams of a better future and finding myself were stronger than my desire to settle down. At 28, I did what most women my age wouldn't do. I marched on to China.

As my MBA graduation drew near in early 2013, I hadn't achieved what I wanted in China and I felt that I needed more time. I told one of my classmates of my dilemma. I also told him of this young man who is waiting for me in Tanzania. At the time, communication between the young man and I wasn't so frequent. I had felt some change. We hadn't seen each other for two years and he had promised to come visit me, which didn't happen. During that time I had a fling with someone else in China. I also felt the same happened to him.

My classmate was of the opinion that this man would not wait for me any longer especially if I wouldn't go back in July 2013 after my graduation. On the other hand, I was a self-paying MBA student and I didn't have enough money to go back to Tanzania in July and return to China in time to register for a PhD in September. Also, my younger sister was getting married in December of the same year. It was only logical to wait till then and travel back home. My classmate also advised me not to say anything about an affair that I had, but of course I told him when we met in Dar after I got back for my sister's wedding. I felt he deserved to know. He always knew I would tell him in case anything like that happened. He would joke about it, on how truthful or open I could be.

Well after talking to my classmate, while still in Wuhan I made a call and communicated my desire to continue with a Ph.D. He wasn't so happy about it but I understood his point of view. When I asked him if he was still interested in the relationship, he said that he had met someone else. He couldn't understand why I wanted to get a PhD. I remember him saying, "So you think you can change the world?" He continued jokingly, "Do you want to be a professor, open a shop in Kariakoo?' (*Kariakoo* is a local market in the city). When we finally met in Dar es Salaam, I could see that a part of him was concerned about me. Once, when we were talking, he looked at me as though I had lost touch with reality. I thought it frightened him to be with someone like me. He needed stability – someone with a job and maybe a strong family support. But I didn't want a job, I supported myself. My dad had retired, and we his children supported him.

In my heart, I knew I was crazy. It was 2013 and I was 30 years old. My younger sister was pregnant with her first child, tying the knot at the end of the year. Almost all of my friends had gotten married and had babies. And there I was in China, chasing a dream that seemed far and blew up a chance with the only man who nearly proposed, at the time.

I admit that there was a time when I was scared. I asked myself, "*Shubi, what are you doing?*" Sometimes, I was scared no one would marry me, an African woman like me who is 'petite in posture', with a PhD and crazy dreams. But I knew I wanted to be truly happy. I wouldn't be happy if I didn't pursue what I felt was right for me. Sometimes, I wished I was the kind of a person that would just be happy to settle for any job and raise babies. I prayed and believed that if God had made me like this, then surely He would provide someone that would be a match for me. He would bring someone that I would be free to share my dreams with because I would know that fully supports me. I thought that to live any other way would be living a lie.

I knew that my family needed this kind of a spirit, to live outside of what is considered normal; not to conform to rules set by the majority. I knew that I wanted the next generation of Kikokos and my children to live in abundance and to know that there are no limits except for what we put for ourselves. And that we are no different from the people who have made it and successful or who are billionaires. I knew that if I died unsuccessful at least I had tried. But I wouldn't give up. And maybe someone in my family or someone else would be inspired by my passion and drive and set out to do the same for their lives and succeed.

In mid-2013, after my third boyfriend in Tanzania told me he met someone else and hence had no more plans of getting married with me. I got into a relationship in Wuhan with a man younger man; let's call him Zamani* who was best friend to Historia*[6] a former boyfriend in Wuhan. I became the kind of woman I would judge. After this experience, I learned to never judge. Zamani and I had a relationship for a bit more than six months. We were almost living together and we never had any major problems. He was matured beyond his age.

---

[6] * Real names have been concealed

At some time in early 2012, I made a vision board of the things I wanted out of life. This was after I had watched *The Secrets documentary* by Rhonda Byrne. One of the things I had on that board was a photo of a bride and groom. I dated the celebration – December 2013. The documentary advised viewers to put this board somewhere where it could be seen frequently. I did as they instructed. But, after some time, I hid it behind my closet. I didn't want people to see it and start asking questions. And for a while, I forgot about it.

The trick about a vision board is not only to put it out in the open but to also work daily towards achieving your goals. You must have daily objectives in the manner that you carry yourself and what you do towards your goals. Placing photos on the board and going on in the direction different from your dreams, doesn't work. December 2013 was my young sister's wedding – not mine as I had "wished" on the vision board. I had written the vision board a year before and forgot about it. Actually, nobody knew about my vision board, until this writing. I seriously think God has a sense of humour or sometimes sends direct messages to save us. This made me stop and analyse what I want and how I should live my life in accordance to my goals.

At the end of 2013, before my travel back home I was changing. I woke up one morning and broke off the relationship with Zamani. I wanted a meaningful relationship that could lead to marriage. My MBA classmate was right when he told me, "This dream you are chasing would not happen in a day. But don't waste your time getting old waiting to achieve it before you start a family."

This wasn't an easy break up because I didn't hate him. We didn't fight nor did we have problems. But I knew the relationship wasn't right. Apart from the fact that he was younger, I knew he didn't want to settle down with me and why would he? The foundation wasn't right. (Most) men don't settle down with women who have had a relationship with their friends.

How did that happen?

A relationship was ending with Historia in Wuhan. Heartaches and lies and on one evening I said "I am going to hurt you". Was I evil? – Yes I think so too. I mean who tells you they are going to hurt you? Well, I did. And guess what? The devil was right there to make sure that my wish comes true. Because I never really had plans to hurt the guy. It was just in the heat of anger and I thought that someone having the thought that someone will hurt them was enough torture on their conscious. And voila! Months later, his friend Zamani becomes interested in me. Of course I was mortified of the idea at first. But the rest is history.

In the secret documentary it was explained that everything you have or that's in your life you are attracting them to you. I could not believe it. Am I attracting meaningless relationships? Are you attracting unfaithful men in your life? – *how?* You become what you think about most and you also attract what you think about most. Also try having standards to what you allow into your life.

From the beginning, it was clear to me that this relationship with Zamani in Wuhan was not going to end anywhere. He was doing his undergraduate degree. Most men would usually think about settling down when they are in the position to provide for the family. Now, was I going to wait until he graduated four years later? And what are the chances that he would still have his eyes only on me? It was not a guarantee! In the meantime, I would be growing older, and more insecure.

After the break up, I read *He is not that into you* by Greg Behrendt and Liz Tuccillo. This book confirmed a lot of worries I had and confirmed that I wasn't going crazy. Men know who they want to settle down with, fast. It doesn't take them two or five years to know. It takes men less than a year to know. They would string you along, but trust me, they know. If they find the love of their lives they usually don't waste time and definitely would not let you go. And wouldn't you want to get married with someone who chose you right away. I mean someone who knew you were the one from the beginning. And not someone that needed convincing for years, while weighing his options and then *finally* chose you.

What did I want? What was my prayer? I didn't want to just have a boyfriend. I prayed to God for someone who wants a wife and not a girlfriend. I also didn't want to start any relationship that didn't involve God from the beginning. I knew the relationship had to be godly, that it shouldn't be my decision but God's. It had occurred to me that most of the time, we start relationships that are doomed from the beginning. It's truly idiotic how we get crushed at the end while all the signs were there, from the start. I no longer had time for that. I was tired.

Also, I had learned that most of my relationships had started with a sexual interaction from the beginning which blurred my decision making. My head would be so clear after a breakup, able to analyse the relationship. And I usually saw how these relationships didn't have a single chance to turn out into anything. Well, sometimes we start out a fling and as time goes, you start thinking maybe a fling could turn to a 'beautiful forever'. Most women are guilty of this. But for most men, they are clear on who they want to marry and who is just a fling. Knowing all that from experience, I wanted something different. I needed clear known intentions right from the beginning. The foundation of a relationship is very important. How you start a relationship matters a lot.

Meeting My Love

He had a crush on me when I was taking my Bachelor's Degree at Mzumbe University. He was a friend of a friend. I never knew about this. He told me about his crush when we started talking. And he reminded me that, it even happened one day, for about few minutes, we were waiting for a friend in a room – just the two of us but we never said a word to each other. And that other time I would stare at him when we passed each other in the campus. I was surprised because honestly I didn't remember all of this. It took about nine years from when we *met* to when he told me about this in 2015.

Through Facebook, he learnt that we share the same birthday – March 8. I truly think that God has a sense of humour, making my husband my birthday mate. When we started communicating (on Facebook), he told me about this. I didn't believe him and I thought men are really creative, coming up with different ways to get close to a girl. So in that way we started chatting and getting to know each other.

We started to communicate frequently in early 2014. We became closer. I started to like him as a friend and would look forward to his messages. It happened at a time when I was building myself and fighting temptations of going back to my old self. We became better friends and in about a year he asked me to go out with him. We started dating in February 2015. How did he ask me out? He asked, "How about we start a serious relationship that leads to marriage?"

When we started communicating, I thought he was interested in me but he never said anything about it. And I never said anything either. I promised myself I wouldn't say anything. Since he is a junior handsome pilot, I knew that he was used to women falling for him and initiating conversation about a potential relationship. I also knew that some men are clever; they would give you all the right signs that they are into you and never take the next step. Most women fall into that trap and instead of a man pursuing us, we start chasing them. I didn't want to cheat myself of the pleasure of having this man express his love for me. And do you know what he said when I asked him why he didn't ask me earlier? He said he was getting to know me and other few girls at the same time in order to decide who was right to settle down with. Imagine if I didn't play it cool? Actually, he said one of the girls proposed to marry him. And he said that made him discredit her.

I was likely to do the same thing if I didn't receive Jesus Christ as my Lord and Savior that same year - March 2, 2014. I would have been desperate and I wouldn't have faith that the right man would come into my life at the right time. I would have approached every man that seemed a bit interested in me and hand myself over for marriage as if it was a business contract. I had put rules for myself:

Rule #1: The next relationship that I was going to get into is with someone who is looking for a wife. Otherwise, it wouldn't have made sense to break up with a 'perfectly' casual relationship only to get into the same kind again.

Rule #2: I needed to involve God before I got into the next relationship. It seemed funny to me that we only involve Him when things don't work out. While we never asked His opinion before we got into a relationship.

Rule #3: To trust God's will for my life. I told God that I would wait and I wouldn't compromise. I wouldn't get into any lesser relationship than that led to marriage. It is not written that every woman must get married. If I was one of them, I told God - let it be.

Rule #4: I was not going to propose to a man. In marriage, you need someone who will stick it out in the rough times – someone who wants to be married to you. Trust me, there is no man who is too polite, who doesn't go for what he wants. Let him do his part. Marriage is already demanding enough, with you adding up, being with someone who partly doesn't want to be with you.

Rule #5: I was tired of casual sex – since I accepted Christ, that couldn't happen. [Hebrews 13:4| NKJV] *Marriage is honourable among all, and the bed undefiled; but fornicators and adulterers God will judge.* I knew this was my shield. Any man who isn't serious will run when you tell them 'no sex till marriage'.

I thank God that my fiancé agreed to 'no sex till marriage'. As I am writing this book we are waiting for the wedding. It is not easy. We have been tempted. But we have prayed after for forgiveness and knew how to stay away from situations that would make it hard for us to stay faithful to our vow. With God's grace, we will be getting married having waited for about a year. Thinking about this, I feel some kind of beautiful warmth in my heart. I never thought I would get the kind of a man that would agree to wait for marriage to have sex. I think it is such a blessing. Whatever you want is out there! You just need to know *what you want*.

During this time, we had read a book called *The Wait* from a Hollywood couple, Devon Franklin and Megan Good who waited till they were married to have sex. This gave us encouragement to push on and commit to be faithful to our decision, which feels like the most alien thing to do in our generation.

I'm truly grateful that Deo supports me fully in all of my pursuits. Writing this book is one of them. I am sure that not all men or husbands would allow their wives to do such a thing. He once joked that it's okay with him if I wanted to be a professor or have two PhDs. Jokes aside, I am blessed to have him and all the support he gives me.

He is my dream come true. God saved me just when I was becoming weak.

I told God, the time is now. You have to save me now. I'm falling. And He did, a month after, Deo asked if I wanted to start a relationship. God saved me. It is not that I was strong enough to pass through temptations even after I had accepted Him as my Lord and Saviour. His grace and mercy saved me. I was going back to fornication, to the old me, to the old boyfriend who I had broken up with knowing clearly that he wasn't going to settle down with me.

Trust me, I have learnt what they say is true that love will come to you when you are totally relaxed and just enjoying yourself and life. When you least expect it. Not by thinking every man you meet, every man who is the least kind to you that he might be Mr Right. That will only delay it to actually happen and instead might send you into the wrong hands.

7. DAD'S PASSING

He remembered that they were but flesh, a wind that passes and comes not again.

Psalm 78:39 |ESV

DREAM CAME TRUE

The dream was so vivid. We were in my dad's funeral at home. Most of our relatives and friends were there, mourning in loud cries. The dream was so real. I woke up crying and sweating. I cried in my room for a long time.

This was around December 2014. It was past midnight and I wasn't alone. This was in Wuhan and I was with Zamani – almost a year after we broke up we started sleeping together again – this lasted only for a while. He didn't understand why I was crying – I couldn't and didn't want to explain. I have a principle: I never talk about something that's really bad. I feel like if I talk about it, I give it roots. The word gets to breathe and would be manifested into life.

I was conflicted. I couldn't understand, why would the Lord speak to me on the day that I was with a man? Why wouldn't God choose the day that I was fasting or when I was closer to Him? Was this dream from God or the devil?

However, I prayed and rebuked the claim on my dad's life. I also got my siblings to join me in fasting and praying together. I didn't tell them about the dream. I didn't want to scare them and I didn't want to give life to the dream.

So, we chose some days in a week and prayed together. The prayers continued each week from then on for a month. My dad's wellbeing was one of the things we were praying for when we were fasting. The song by Donnie McClurkin called 'Great is your Mercy' was like a theme song for me – day in, day out through this whole time.

After this month of prayers, I really got peace in my heart that everything is okay. It wasn't until Easter when my siblings told me they had lunch with dad and he told them that he didn't want us to bury him in Bukoba – this is his origin and where his parents are buried. Instead dad said that he should be buried near our mother when he died.

"I should be buried near my wife". That's what he said.

Everyone was surprised to hear this and they tried to ask him why he was talking like this. It's not good to talk about death. He replied politely, "No I'm just saying I think it's better not to travel all the way to the village." My step mother and the rest thought that maybe our dad was still grieving. And of course, he was, his very good friend had died a month before. He had a stroke and died a few days after. We thought, maybe, that was why he was thinking about death. When they told me about this conversation, I got very scared and remembered the dream that I hadn't told anyone.

I would get jumpy every time I received a message from dad. I would make sure that I responded to his texts on time. We now think that he knew his time had arrived. Exactly two weeks after Easter, dad passed away. In a month's time, prior to his passing, he had called many of his relatives to greet them. They would recall their conversation with him when they came for the funeral.

Later on, I realised that the message was from God because after the dream I got closer to Him with fasting and praying and I was able to stay away from any sexual temptations. Also, in a way God was telling me that He does what He does because He is God. It is not because of the cleanliness of my heart. He is a gracious God. Grace means receiving undeserved favour, not because we deserve it, not because we are so holy. The sun shines for both good and bad people and that's how God is. He has faith in you and waits for you to come to Him and He forgives you every time you fall. He is a merciful God.

We had always prayed for dad to be saved and accept Christ for as long as I can remember. The last time I saw him was in March 2014 when I had gone home for holidays. I asked him, "Dad, maybe you should give your life to Jesus." My dad was a Muslim. He replied politely, "But we consider Jesus as a prophet," and I just said 'okay'. I didn't press him further. I didn't want to upset him. Now I regret that I didn't try harder.

A Peaceful Death

During this time, May 2015 I was in Hong Kong. This was the first time I was meeting Deo after two months of dating. Prior our meeting we communicated mostly through FaceTime. I remember when I was leaving my room in Wuhan I was telling God please talk to me. Let me know if it's ok to get into this relationship.

That Saturday afternoon, I was chatting with dad. He told me that he would go to a wedding later that day and he promised to send me photos afterwards.

The following day, Sunday morning in Hong Kong – that means in Dar es Salaam was past midnight – five hours behind China's time zone. My younger brother called me with the devastating news. The day I was supposed to land back in Wuhan from Hong Kong I was landing in Dar es Salaam for my dad's funeral.

INCUBATED IN CHINA

Dad's death was fast. When he died, he was happy. He was at a wedding, in a suit. Surrounded by people he loved. On entering in the wedding reception hall they – my dad, step mother, young brother and his buddy – joined the celebrations dancing. And soon, food was served.

I was told that before they started eating, my step mother asked the waiter to take a photo of two of them – my dad and her. A few spoons later, my dad had a sip of water and was choked by it. As he was trying to clear his throat, he asked my step mom to escort him to the bathroom. She threw her arms around my dad and started walking with him. But before they got there, my dad slipped and fell to the floor. My younger brother and his friend saw this and rushed to help. They thought that he had fainted.

After being resuscitated at the hospital, the medical officers confirmed that there was no heartbeat. My family couldn't believe this, they wanted to have another opinion. My younger sister and her husband had also arrived at the hospital. They were on their way to the wedding when they received the shocking news.

After a long discussion with the doctors and efforts to resuscitate our dad failed, my family agreed to sign the papers to transfer dad to the mortuary. And that was it. My step mother thought they were transferring dad to another hospital for treatment, after they had put him in an ambulance. Only to find out they are outside the mortuary and that's when reality hit her. Dad was really gone.

We are thank God that His mercy and grace prepared us. Because of the vision He had given me, we fasted and prayed together, it had never happened before that time. God answered our prayers because our dad didn't suffer. It was quick and he had prepared himself. During this last month, he was praying a lot. He would often give me a word of wisdom, the kind that a man gives at his deathbed. He told me to make sure that our youngest sister – Nasra studies hard. He wanted her to graduate from university so that all his kids had good education.

When we were texting each other, I thought he was worried for nothing. I told him to relax and I assured him that Nasra will be okay. As we were conversing through text messages, I was walking in Wuhan around the university and I came around the street I like – the one that has plane tall trees on each side of the street. I took a photo of these trees and sent it to dad. I told him how I love the street and the trees because it's very peaceful. But he didn't make any comment about the trees. He just kept on texting about Nasra. So I had to assure him that we will make sure that she did well in school. I was kind of surprised, a little hurt and wondered why he didn't say anything about my trees. Now I think that, maybe the trees and its peacefulness spoke to him more than I knew or intended to communicate.

When he passed away, it had been a year since I last saw him. The guilt and pain was excruciating. I was supposed to go back home during the winter holiday in January. But I postponed my trip because of a job I got. And I thought I would go in the summer during a longer holiday. But he passed away in early May 2015. Ever since then, I have promised myself to always go back home at least once a year, no matter how broke I am.

Dad's passing brought a lot of life changing questions to my mind about the judgment day and concerning hell and heaven. I know that through Jesus Christ we get salvation and forgiveness of sin which can make us worthy of heaven. But then, I thought about the pagans, atheist or people of other religions that don't believe in Jesus. Do they *all* go to hell?

I got an insight that entering heaven is by the grace of God. Even believers fall short of the glory of God and it is only by His grace that we can be made righteous. Ephesians 2:8 says for by grace are ye saved through faith; and that not of yourselves: *it is* the gift of God.

God is just and fair. He would judge everyone based on the responses to the knowledge of the truth that was available to each of us. For example, He will not judge pagans the same as He would judge believers who accepted His law. But also it's important to note that even people who don't have faith in Christ know and are convicted in their hearts about wrong and right. Their conscience testifies against them when they act against the natural laws in their hearts or their accepted norms in the community. On the judgment day God will judge the purposes and secrets of people's hearts.

For as many as have sinned without law will also perish without law, and as many as have sinned in the law will be judged by the law (for not the hearers of the law are just in the sight of God, but the doers of the law will be justified; for when Gentiles, who do not have the law, by nature do the things in the law, these, although not having the law, are a law to themselves, who show the work of the law written in their hearts, their conscience also bearing witness, and between themselves their thoughts accusing or else excusing them in the day when God will judge the secrets of men by Jesus Christ, according to my gospel. [Romans 2:12-16 | NKJV]

INCUBATED IN CHINA

LIFE IS NOTHING BUT A MOMENT

The reality that we are only here for a moment sunk in with the passing of my father. I mean, just seeing him getting old was phenomenal to me. Not long ago he was strong playing volleyball and basketball with us. He was a tall man, about 1.80 metres and had a body of an athlete. Seeing him getting old, becoming weak because of the stroke – dad had an ischemic stroke on the left side of his body in late 2010, was a reminder that we are not getting younger and time passed only so quickly.

In those few minutes before he passed away, he was taking photos with his wife. This was scary. How do you recognise a dying man?

What I learned was that we always feel like we have time to do this or that. We feel like we have all the time in the world, and at some point in life, we think that we will accomplish a great thing. But the reality is that we don't have time. Whatever you want to do now is the perfect time to do it. The things you do daily those are the things that make who you are and eventually are the things which we will remember you by. That is your history.

Dad's death was so humbling to me. You don't know

what will happen tomorrow. Be happy when you have been given a chance to wake up. Rejoice and be happy. In fact, I have become more grateful, after dad's passing, especially when I wake up in the morning. I pull up my curtains, I look outside – greeted by the sunshine and beautiful trees and I thank the Lord for another chance with life. God trusts you to do better in every day that you are alive.

It is good to plan things ahead and be excited about tomorrow. But always remember to add in your sentence *"If the Lord wills, we will . . ."* so that you don't become too arrogant. Everything we do is because of His grace upon us.

Now listen, you who say, "Today or tomorrow we will go to this or that city, spend a year there, carry on business and make money." Why, you do not even know what will happen tomorrow. What is your life? You are a mist that appears for a little while and then vanishes. Instead, you ought to say, "If it is the Lord's will, we will live and do this or that." As it is, you boast in your arrogant schemes. All such boasting is evil. [James 4:13-16 | NIV]

Above is my Father and His granddaughter, Leanne Kimberly. From left below Ibrahim, Mama Nasra, Dad, Leanne and my brother in law, and Siima.

This is the last photo I sent to my Dad before he passed away, showing him the Plane trees in Mafanshang East Campus at Wuhan University of Technology.

8. MOM AND DAD – LESSONS LEARNT

"Love is how you stay alive, even after you are gone."

Mitch Albom

UNSHAKABLE FAITH

I started writing this chapter on the day that marked 17 years since my mom passed away. Siima reminded us about the anniversary with a text in our siblings group on WhatsApp. Laying on my bed, my head facing the ceiling and legs pulled to my chest, I was taken back in memory lane. I thought of how blessed we are to have had her as our mother. Tears started flowing down to my ears as I thought of her life near death.

Then I heard birds singing outside my balcony – my dorm room was just a bedroom with a balcony – through which I got to enjoy a breathtaking view of nature. There were a lot of trees and beautiful birds that landed on them. As I looked onto the direction of the beautiful distraction from my thoughts I realized my curtains were still closed. I was still under the duvet covers since it was a slightly cold morning. It was the beginning of spring in Wuhan. While still under the covers, I pulled my laptop and started writing. I thought it was a perfect day to write as I reminisced with gratitude, wonder and joy about my mom's life.

Here we go.

I remember clearly when my mom told me that she will go to the hospital to get her breasts tested. This was in late 1996 when I was in Form One. It was just the two of us in her bedroom. She said she had a swelling in one of her breasts.

"Could it be cancer?" I asked with concerns.

"Shubi!!" she said.

That's all she said as she was preparing to go out. I don't know where that came from because at that time I didn't know what cancer was. If I knew cancer, then I wouldn't have dared to ask that question. Somehow I always felt like I had jinxed her just by asking her that. Aunt Christina (my mother's younger sister), she later told us that mom had told her that she suspects a swelling on her breast when she was breastfeeding her last born – my brother Ibrahim who was born in 1988.

I remember how after she got the results, she started getting counselling at the church she was attending. I think that's when she decided that she was not going to remove her left breast, the affected one. It was okay in the beginning. She continued going to work as usual. She was a nursing teacher at the time, at the biggest national referral hospital in the country – Muhimbili National

Hospital – which wasn't far from our house. She used to walk to work. But things weren't really the same.

Fast forward a year and a half later, the cancer had become so severe and had been eating away the affected breast. The pain had spread throughout her upper arm, shoulder and upper back.

It reached a point that my mother could not bathe herself. It hurt me to see her this way. This is when I got into close contact with the disease and how it can eat your body away piece by piece. The breast skin was bare open. It was all pink, filled with pus. As I cleaned the breast some parts of her skin would come out with the sterilized cloth that I used for cleaning. It was extremely painful, I could see it, and I could feel it with every fleeting touch of the disinfectant touching her skin. But worse was the thought, the psychological torture, I would think, that she had to see part of her body decaying while she was still living.

She had lost a lot of weight at that time and after a while, the second breast started to be infected as well. If am not mistaken, its morphine injections that she used for her pain in every four hours. The pain was too strong. She received a dozen of these medicines to treat herself at home because she was not admitted. I think they allowed this knowing that she was a nurse by profession and also her friend who was a nurse lived in the same apartment building.

The medicine was in a little see through glass, maybe 6 centimetres in length and 2 centimetres in width. It had a thin neck which we would break the neck and take out the liquid with a syringe. I remember how mom used to call us to help her break the neck before giving herself shots on her thigh. There was a time her thighs were swollen and she had to teach me and sometimes – when I wasn't around my younger sister Siima how to give her an injection. I remember this clearly, she said, "Divide the buttock in four parts and you should inject the lower left part." I still can remember the feeling when the needle passed through her flesh every time I gave her an injection.

At the age of 16, I was nursing my mother, giving her injections and giving her infected body a bath. Looking back and thinking about this, I acknowledge that it was all God's deeds. I don't know how we got the strength to do all that. I remember how mum would call me when I was watching 'Days of Our Lives' on TV with my siblings. "*Shubi njoo*," she would call out for me to go to her since it was time for her injection. But my childish self would sometimes reply, "Mom, please wait just a minute," so I could finish a favorite scene.

OBEDIENCE TO GOD

My mother was always happy, cheerful and playful. She was very beautiful. Her skin was light in tone, her hair was about 16 inches long and naturally soft. And she short was about 1.53 metres. For some time, towards the end of her life, she kept her long hair natural. My grandmother once said that in the village where my mother grew up, people would call her *'mzungu'* which is what we call Caucasians – white people in Kiswahili, because of her physical appearance.

My dad had a second wife, but we never thought this bothered my mom. It wasn't until her friend asked me if I thought that mom was bothered, and then I started wondering. This was after mom had passed away. Her question got me thinking for many years. I started wondering why mom never left dad, especially after I started dating myself. I wondered how she managed to be cool about it to the point us her children didn't notice any strife or sadness. I had also started to observe how most marriages end up in divorce. Then I read this *"For I hate divorce!" says the Lord, the God of Israel.* [Malachi 2:16a NLT] and figured this must have been the reason. My mom always considered dad as her husband until her death, although he had a second wife. She was always happy, always wore her face with joy. It's truly unbelievable. I feel this is very difficult for any woman or wife. I often wonder how she did it and I arrive to one answer, her fellowship with God was her secret. As long as your husband lives if you get another you are an adulterer. [Luke 16:18 NLT]

Middle of 1990s, mom travelled to the US for a nursing teachers training. Our neighbours (who were Indians) had a garage. Mom bought a second hand car from them, after she came back from the US and dad fixed it. It was a Datsun pickup that my dad would use all the time. He would drive to work and to his other home every night. He came home every day and spent time with us as a family. We would play sports, either basketball or volleyball each week. He would also help us with homework and had dinner together.

Before cancer came into our lives, Saturdays were 'Kids in the kitchen' day. We would cook all the delicious meals such as chapatti, roasted liver, fries, salads and so on. My mom had a naughty laughter. When she laughed, you couldn't help but join her in laughing, unless the joke was on you. Then, it wouldn't be so funny. It was also a custom for her to go for door to door evangelism. When we asked her where she was going, she would answer, "I am going to fish people." And she would be laughing because at that time, we really didn't understand what she meant. To say that she was 'fishing people' was funny to us. But she was being obedient to God – as Christians we are supposed to bear fruits. *When you produce much fruit, you are my true disciples. This brings great glory to my Father.* [John 15:8 NLT] But when she was ill, all she could do was lay in bed. Sometimes she would rest in the living room. This happened for about a year when she was seriously ill until she passed away.

People used to come visit her while some would just send their love. It was amazing to see how all that came, left strengthened by her. I remember Mama Dainess who was a next door neighbour once said, "This is amazing, instead of being the one who is giving her strength, I am the one receiving encouragement from her the patient."

I never saw her cry when she was sick. It almost feels like she was disconnected from the pain. On her last day on earth, I was scared for her. She was in a lot of pain. I wanted to know what was in her heart. I wanted to make sure that she was still holding on to Christ. I clearly remember while sitting by her side, I asked her, "Mom, do you still believe in God?" She looked at me straight in the eye with a look that said, how you could ask me that?

Then she uttered, "Shubi! Yes, of course."

Although she was always fighting, I could sense that that day was not the same. She was in enormous pain. Many people had come to see her that day and mom couldn't settle down. She couldn't even eat. We brought her some light food but she only ate a little. She was restless on her bed. I had already given her a shot to calm down the pain but that didn't help. One of her long-time friend, who was also living in the same apartment building, asked my mother, "Ruth what can I do for you?" and my mom cried out: "My children, my children"

In the room was *bibi* (my grandmother), *Mama Mdogo* (my mom's younger sister) and some other Aunts. Although it was already late, my father was called. I think they realised that my mother's condition was worse that night. Dad used to share his time between his two homes. After they called him he came back. I later found out that dad decided to go to his other home after staying with mom for a while, since it was getting pretty late. My mom passed away when he left, and they had to call for him to come back again. And it was him who woke us up that morning to break the news to us.

For the longest time, I was angry at my father for this. It was until after he got a stroke that I cried and I prayed that God should forgive him and heal him and give him more life on earth. It is because of how it happened that I battled this fear of dying alone. But I got over that when I realized that my mother was not alone when she died. The most important presence you need when you pass along to the other side is your faith and being in peace with your God.

My mom would always say that you should invest in heaven. I remember withdrawing money from her bank account on her behalf when she was bedridden. She would fill the deposit slips at home. Mom would take 10 percent of the money, put it in an envelope and give her friend to deliver it to the church as her tithe offering. Mom would often say that the money you give will be used to build your house in heaven. She would say that while some people would have beautiful mansions in heaven, others would have normal houses. This bold act touched my life. Even when she was sick on her bed, she never departed from the ways of the Lord.

Mom lost a lot weight and her hair too. Whenever we

used to want to play with her hair, before she got sick, she would refuse. I always thought she had a sensitive scalp because she would complain that it hurts to touch her hair. But when she was sick, she would let us comb her hair and braid her with no complains. I figured that she didn't mind anymore and that the pain she felt exceeded the discomfort of touching her sensitive scalp. Or maybe she wanted to cherish every moment with us.

I remember one day, a short while before she died, she wanted us to go for Ice cream. She was feeling better on that day. It was just the four of us – mom and her kids. We walked to the nearest Azam Bakhresa Ice cream parlour. That was the last time we went out and had fun with her. I remember her looking at us attentively while we were enjoying our ice creams. Somehow, we had less care of how big that moment was. We were just children enjoying ice cream. I wonder if she knew that the end had come for her and that she wanted to share with us this one last happy time.

Although I knew cancer was a deadly disease, mom had me and all of us convinced that she wasn't dying. I thought that if all it needed was faith to get healed then surely healing was all hers. You know, at one point, I was sure that my mom would be healed from cancer and be okay again. She was so sure of that as well. There is this verse in the Bible that we read with her along with many other verses. And this was the verse:

[Psalm 118:17 NIV] *I will not die but live, and will proclaim what the LORD has done.*

Years after her passing, I was still confused on how God could let her die. She believed in Him through it all. I asked myself what was the meaning of it all. Did she lose? Was God angry with her and that's why He did not heal her?

Sometimes, I wonder if she was ever scared. But of course she must have been, I think. But if she was, she never showed or expressed it to us or anyone else. My mom was very strong. I know for certain that there is no way she managed that by herself. It was her faith in the Lord that pulled her through. Mom had what my siblings and I call 'the unwavering faith', every day, all the time. It was so strong that she had us believe in her recovery too.

I can't imagine how we would have handled it if she wasn't strong. Life would have been a nightmare for us. Come to think of it, she probably didn't want to put us through that and that's why she asked for strength. She would call us three to her room on numerous occasions and say that she was in pain. She would ask us to sing for her.

Damu ya Yesu,

Damu ya Yesu,

Damu ya Yesu

Husafisha kabisa.

Na nguvu za shetani zimeshindwa.

Na nguvu za shetani zimeshindwa

Na nguvu za shetani zimeshindwa

Katika Jina la Yesu

Na sisi tunaimba Haleluya.

Na sisi tunaimba Haleluya

Na sisi tunaimba Haleluya

Asifiwe mwokozi.

It was a song that called on the blood of Jesus,

rebuked the powers of satan, and praised the name of Jesus.

This was her favorite song. We would sing it over and over again until she felt better and the pain would go away. Once she calmed down, we would stop singing. There was also another song that she liked, *God will make a way* by Don Moen. It was a radio cassette that we would sing along with. The lyrics of the chorus said, *God will make a way where it seems to be no way, He works in ways we cannot see, He will make a way for me, He will be my guide, draw me closer to His side. With love and strength for each new day, He will make a way, He will make a way.*

Sometimes, I wish that she should have written a book or kept a diary so we could find out what was really going on in her head at the time of her sickness. But as times goes by, I get these revelations or 'Aha!' moments on what must have been for her and I learn. Then I think, perhaps it is better this way than if she had kept a diary.

On my mom's last breath she said "*Ninyanyue, ninyanyue*" in Kiswahili, which means *pick me up*. Aunt Christina said people in the room thought she was talking to them and went to help her. That's how she passed on to the other side.

My mother passed away late March, 1999 at a young age of 43. I had just turned 16, Siima was 13 and Ibrahim was 11 years old. She left us at the age when we needed a mother the most. Our dad had a second wife, he could have taken us to live with her which could have made our lives worse. Mom knew all this, yet she was very calm and peaceful during the whole time of her illness. I usually think about this and I see how only her faith in God could have allowed her to behave that way.

For the longest time, I didn't communicate much with God. I didn't pray. I just didn't understand. I was quiet. I couldn't understand. Wasn't God supposed to save the good people? I mean my mom had so much faith and she never complained once till the end. We recited all these verses from the Bible together about the promises of God being the salvation and her rescue; that she will not die but proclaim the good works of God. But I have realized that *He is God*, and when we pray we should add "let your will be done". I hope that my mom is still living on in heaven and this book will proclaim the good works that the Lord has done in hers and our lives because He is forever faithful.

At 16, I had experienced at close range, a strong example of how to walk with God. But I only gave my life to Christ when I was 31. I think that apart from other things, I was scared of making that decision earlier on in life because of my mom's experience. I knew if you give your life to Christ your life is not yours. You should be happy to serve the Lord and His Kingdom even if it meant to die. You should be ready to totally surrender your life to God and serve His ways. *For if we live, we live to the Lord; and if we die, we die to the Lord. Therefore, whether we live or die, we are the Lord's. [Romans 14:8 | NKJV]* and Philippians 1:21 | NKJV says, For to me, to live is Christ, and to die is gain.

That kind of commitment or declaration scared me. I would also think, *what if I fail?,* I was scared of being so highly committed to God then fall, and worse enough drag down other people who believed Christ through you. I also knew, as soon as you declare to give your life to Jesus, it is as if you have declared war against Satan and his works. He will not stop throwing darts at you to bring you down from your commitment with God. And I thought how God would sometimes allow His people to be tested, something like Job's story. But that was me thinking like child and blurred by fear with the devil. *So he answered, "Do not fear, for those who are with us are more than those who are with them." [2 Kings 6:16 | NKJV]*

Sacrifice

After living in the same house for about five years, dad had an announcement to make to the three of us. "Mama Nasra and I will be moving to another house," dad said. We were all devastated to hear this. I couldn't understand what was going on. We wanted to know why this was happening. And dad said, "I want everyone to know where they belong, so that there won't be any problems when I am not around."

So that was it. They moved out after a few months and the five of us started living alone. That included Nasra, Ibrahim, Siima, a maid and I.

Mom and dad had bought the plot where the house we were living in was built, back in the 1980s. When mum was sick, we were still living in the company's apartments in Upanga. She had told me to make sure that dad finished the house in Tabata, which he did. We moved in when his employer decided to stop providing accommodation to his employees.

The house in Tabata wasn't completely done. However, the house that dad and Mama Nasra moved into in Chanika was even worse. Dad had started building another house all over again. It was further away from the city. My dad had built three houses in his life. The first one was for our step mother – the one who was around when my mum was alive. As a Muslim man, his faith allowed him to have more than one wife.

When my mum passed away, the three of us lived with dad. He would share his time between us and our step mother. We lived separately; she had her own house and we lived with dad in the apartment that his employer had provided. He never had a child with our first step mother. For about a year after we had moved to Tabata, in 2002 dad introduced us to our second stepmother and our younger sister, Nasra. I remember dad taking us to meet Nasra a few months after her birth. When Nasra was about two years old, they moved in with us in Tabata. And later, my dad remained with only one wife – Mama Nasra.

When he announced that he was moving from Tabata to another house. This was a third house he was building at the time when he already retired, where he moved to with Mama Nasra. Although they had a bigger plot of about two acres, their house was smaller and it was of poor quality compared to ours.

Every time I think of this, I can't help but get

emotional. This is the greatest selfless act I have experienced in my life – from my father. When they moved to Chanika those areas hadn't even been connected to electricity poles or services. I always think of the successful life that he has had as a civil engineer in one of the biggest corporations in the country and then to end up in that kind of a house after his retirement. It is both heart - breaking and so heroic.

Dad sacrificed moving out so he could make things right. But how many people would have done that? How many would care about what happens after he is gone. Although, the truth is, we wouldn't have refused to live with our stepmother. We had already lived together for about five years. They moved in with us in 2004. I think it was dad's way of making things right and showing respect to our mother, whom they started building the house together. He gave us the house and chose to start over.

In Chanika, our dad enjoyed small farming on his 2-acres land. He cultivated bananas (from Bukoba where he came from), cassava, maize, mangoes and oranges. Before he retired, he would say that he would go back to the village and farm once he retired. We are comforted to know that at least he was happy to do the same in Chanika. When dad moved out, my siblings and I each contributed an amount to fence the house we lived in. And just like that, we started being independent.

UNCONDITIONAL LOVE

My mom taught me that it doesn't matter what the other does, there is no reason strong enough for you to let go and lose the connection. The devil knows the blessings we have by just being in peace with your siblings or relatives or with others. *How wonderful and pleasant it is when brothers live together in harmony! For harmony is as precious as the anointing oil that was poured over Aaron's head, that ran down his beard and onto the border of his robe. Harmony is as refreshing as the dew from Mount Hermon that falls on the mountains of Zion. And there the Lord has pronounced his blessing, even life everlasting.* [Psalms 133:1-3 | NLT] That's why the devil wants to steal blessings from us by instilling pride, unforgivingness and fault finding among us.

My mother taught me to forgive quickly, I am glad that my siblings forgive me too and we are able to have a relationship that can withstand anything through the fear of God and believing in love, which is a command from God – loving one another.

Through the course of time, especially after I committed my life to Jesus Christ, I have been training myself to practice the same love towards other people as well. In the beginning it was difficult, you always get the urge to get back at someone for what wrong they have done. I don't want to look stupid for being the forgiving one, I would think. I remember debating within myself when someone did me wrong. I would ask myself, *"So what should my response be now?"* The answer would be *"Always choose love."* Repaying good for bad is so refreshing and freeing plus it's a command from the Almighty God.

I have learned that it becomes easier to love when you don't care about the response of the one you are showing love to. You might be tested to retreat and go into coldness instead of showing love. If you do that, then, they win. Especially when you are helping someone never expect anything in return. *And whatever you do, do it heartily, as to the Lord and not to men.* [Colossians 3:23| NKJV] Do it for God's glory! When you help someone they shouldn't even remember your name, they should remember your God.

It's important we know that we show love not only by our words and actions but it could be as simple as our facial expression towards others. When you don't love it shows – *faces don't lie*. I once experienced a sister from church she would always look at me with disgust. I would always smile back at her. When this happens I would pray. *Lord please make them happy* – but never return an unfriendly look for one. Be even more kind. They need it the most. I know it's hard to be happy for someone when you are not happy yourself. I have experienced this. But that's when you make deliberate choices to love and be cheerful. From *Battlefield of the Mind* [7] we learn that there is no need to be jealous or envy or comparing and competing with one another. This is because God has a unique plan for each of us. I also got another priceless lesson from Harv Eker in *Secret of the Millionaire Mind* whereby whenever I see something I like or someone successful, I bless them and be happy for them.

When you love even those who hate you, you make them wonder. *Is this woman crazy? Maybe stupid? Or a pretender?* I must admit, sometimes I smile when haters openly get confused when I don't reciprocate or even show that I notice the offense. They will be waiting for a day when show your 'real' self. Disappoint them each time – this brings glory to God and it heals. And maybe you can win them to the other side. There is nothing we need more

---

[7] 2011, Joyce Meyer. Battlefield of the Mind. Winning the Battle in your Mind. Page 257 -263

in this world right now like love. *But love your enemies, do good to them, and lend to them without expecting to get anything back. Then your reward will be great, and you will be children of the Most High, because he is kind to the ungrateful and wicked. 36 Be merciful, just as your Father is merciful. [Luke 6:35-36 NIV]*

CONFIDENCE

The boy and I were shaking, afraid of what he might do because he seemed angry to the point that he was also shaking. Of course he would be angry. He found us together at the summit of our apartment building; this was maybe around eight evening time. He asked us what were we doing but never waited for the answer. And he ordered me to go down back inside the house; we lived on the ground floor of a three storey building apartment. Everything happened within fraction of seconds.

I expected a beating after this. Dad had beaten me once in my life, in primary school, when I went to church with my friends without his permission. He always said that as long as we were under his roof and under aged, we would follow his religion until when we could decide for ourselves. To my surprise, he got into the house and just went into his room. He didn't say anything to me regarding what had just happened. Nor did he say anything on the following day. He just had an angry face. This was torture. On the second day after the incident, I called him while he was at work. We had a landline phone at the house. And I asked to talk to him when he came home.

When he returned in the evening, I knocked on his door and asked if it was okay to come in. I found him lying on bed on his back. Behind his bed there was a table near the door, I sat on the table.

"You wanted to talk?" he asked me while looking away. I thought that he thought that I was a bad girl. That's what I said to him. I don't remember the rest. But what I do remember is how calm he was in his response. He said that I was an intelligent girl and that boys would only waste my time.

"Work hard in school, boys will always be there," he said. And that was it. I was dismissed. He didn't beat me to death like I imagined. He didn't even tell me, "I never want to see you with that boy again." But in my heart I knew I had to watch out. I didn't want to disappoint him. Through this incident, I felt the pressure that was on him as a single parent. Maybe, at that moment, he might have wished that mom was there to handle this situation.

I think it was very courageous of me to ask dad to accompany me to the same boy's house some months later to deliver a birthday cake I had made. And he did. Dad drove me to his house. He even went in his house and greeted the boy's mother. Maybe I wanted to get his approval and make him a little relaxed on the whole situation. It was somehow scary to think that he agreed to go with me. *Why did he agree?* – I don't know. I was in secondary school at the time and this was my first boyfriend. I was making up jokes in my head, thinking that maybe dad had agreed to go so he would know the boy's home. Then, he could come and kill him, in case he got me pregnant. Anyways, I felt like my dad trusted me a lot. I felt the urge to make it known to him that I am trustworthy.

I think that building children's confidence is a process; one that is more vital when they are younger. Something else happened around the same time during junior high school that proved my dad's support. I knew that he had my back, a knowledge that helped build confidence in myself. This was when I wanted to become a movie director. I had started writing a movie script and I started looking for the cast to fit my play. I made an advertisement and placed in a few secondary schools in the city. I got quite a good response and I was able to connect with more people with same passion. One of them was Paul Mashauri who went on and became an actor, producer, an entrepreneur and inspirational speaker.

The play didn't come to fruition, unfortunately. But one significant thing that did happen, apart from the connections I made, was the fact that my dad was right there by my side, interviewing those who wanted to be part of the cast. This image will always stay with me. We had set up tables and chairs at the summit for the interview. Can you imagine that he believed in me and didn't think I was *crazy*? He made time from his busy schedule to be there for me. He never doubted me nor questioned how a teenager will make a movie bearing in mind all the resources that were needed. This gave me confidence that there was nothing that I couldn't do. My ideas and dreams are valid.

As I approached my late teenage years, sometime between 2000 and 2001, I interned as a presenter at one of famous radio stations in Tanzania. I thank my friend Austin Makani, who has become more than a friend but a brother to me and my siblings as well. He introduced me to the radio's management. And because of Austin, dad felt comfortable to let me go with yet another dream of mine. I am grateful for Austin. Whenever I was out of line, he would look at me straight into my eyes, even if he never said anything, I knew what he meant. I remember his stare across a crowded nightclub. He somehow kept me in check.

I started out being a co-presenter. Later, I managed a show on my own called the Hotmix on Friday night from 11 to 12 midnight, if I remember correctly. I was an 'okay presenter'. I made many mistakes. I remember one day the host for lunch time show wasn't present and I covered for her. That day I forgot to put up the volume after an advertisement. There were a few seconds of silence and my boss came storming in the studio, fuming.

I'm glad the radio management gave me a chance to practice and their willingness to nurture young talents. During this time I got to know many people including the intelligent and eloquent Fina Mango. I used to adore and admire her strength, beauty and poise – I still do. I also got to know some famous Tanzanian musicians such as Lady Jaydee and Ray C. Gerald Hando was an IT manager at the time. He later on became a household name and one of the most famous morning show radio personalities. I would be an ungrateful human being if I didn't mention that he has been a great influence in my life to my mental growth and confidence – at the time I needed it the most.

When I was almost getting the hang of radio presenting, unfortunately, I got to give it up as my dad thought I had to concentrate more on my upcoming A level exams. I'm grateful that my dad accepted my request to practice at the radio station, and do the night shows. Although the office car returned me home after the show, I still think he had so much confidence in me. Sometimes, I would go party after the show if I knew that dad was not home that night, on nights that he would sleep over at our step mother's.

I believe that giving your kids a chance to be able to make their own mistakes is part of being a good parent. Parents act as a buffer so their children know they are trusted and secure, knowing that whenever they fall they can fall back on their parents' support. Children will never learn how to walk on their own if parents are always carrying them. And it's guaranteed that parents won't always be there whenever children make a decision. They should be trained to make their own decisions. *Train up a child in the way he should go, And when he is old he will not depart from it.* [Proverbs 22:6 |NKJV] Above all else asking the grace of God to cover your children even when you are not there this is perhaps the most important of all.

In her book, 'What I wish I knew when I was 20. A Crash Course on Making Your Place in the World', Tina Seeling [8], talks about permissions and courage we get around us to be great.

> *When I got my paper back a week or so later a note written on top said, "Tina, you think like a scientist." At that moment I became a scientist. I was just waiting for someone to acknowledge my enthusiasm – and to give me permission to pursue my interests. We are all powerfully influenced by messages around us.*

One day, in a casual conversation, my dad suggested that I aim to pursue a PhD. I wonder if what he said registered as permission. Remember to always speak positive things in your own life and to those around you. You will never know how a tremendous influence you could be to someone else. *The tongue has the power of life and death.* [Proverbs 18:21a | NLT]

---

[8] Tina Seeling, 2009. What I wish I knew when I was 20. A Crash Course On Making Your Place In The World. pg 105

SENSE OF HUMOR

Dad was a kind man and hospitable to everyone. All our friends loved him. He had a sense of humor, a way to ease situations and make them more bearable. I remember the last joke he made with me just weeks before he passed. His blood pressure was always high and his doctors were looking into different ways to make it better. We were all worried about him.

I asked him over a text message, "Dad what's wrong?" He replied that nothing was wrong. He was taking his medication as usual. He was even exercising. Apart from a limp on his left leg, which he got after he had the stroke, dad was fit. He went to the gym regularly and took long walks to help his leg recover. He always had a strong athletic body.

Sometimes, dad would come to Tabata and spend a few days there, especially if he had a doctor's appointment coming up. He was in Tabata a few weeks before he died. While there, he went to a football pitch not far from our house to exercise in the morning with Ibrahim, my younger brother. While he was doing sit ups, some young people there started teasing my dad. They were amazed that he was that strong. Perhaps this is because he would always limp. Ibrahim told us this story and that dad told those young men, "It's just this leg. Otherwise, I could compete in a marathon with you guys." And they all laughed.

As we were chatting, dad told me that he is exercising and taking medication. "I don't know what these doctors want. Maybe they want me to be Mr. September." I think he was implying about those young and muscular models. I laughed so hard. I am sure that he was laughing too on the other side. Whenever he told a joke he would laugh too.

He was also good at telling stories. He would repeat these stories time to time when we were younger; stories of his life in the village or when he was a new guy in a big city. And if you took a long time in the kitchen, he would bring up a story about a mother with her kids:

> *This mother didn't have food that night. And her kids were very hungry. So she took stones and started boiling them in the pot. The kids would ask, "Mum, when is the food going to be ready?" Their mother would say, "Wait, it's still cooking." This would go on until the kids got tired and slept.*

When we were eating ice creams, he would tell us about

the first time he ate an ice cream cone. How he didn't know that the biscuit was also supposed to be eaten. When he finished eating the ice cream, he threw away the biscuit. When he saw his friends eating the biscuit that's when he learnt how its properly done. We would crack up laughing every time he told this story.

When we couldn't understand why we were unable to afford something, he would tell us a story about when he wanted a new school bag. His father, our grandfather, was a farmer. After one harvest season, my grandfather gave my dad the harvest to sell in the local market. When my dad brought home the money he got, our grandfather didn't take the money from him. He told him to use the money to buy what he needed for school. Dad bought everything he needed, but the money wasn't enough for a new bag. He needed one since he was preparing to go to college. He came back asking for more money. But grandfather told him, "My son you know how much we have made and all the money we had was given to you." He was told to take the old but still strong embossed tin trunk.

Dad recalled running to the next village crying to his aunt that his dad didn't want to buy him a new bag. His aunt gave him the money for a new bag. He bought a luggage which had a cover made of hard paper that was in style at that time. And he took off to college. On his way to college, the new luggage was put on top of the bus as it was customary in those days. Unfortunately, it started raining along the journey. His luggage was almost damaged and his belongings got wet when he arrived. My dad would tell us that that was childish because our grandparents had given him all they could.

On the day before his departure to college his mother gave him some cassava wrapped in banana leaves, a traditional way of packaging food that is still used in Bukoba – our father's origin. But as young people are, we don't always appreciate the homemade food especially if we have to eat in front of our peers. I think that maybe he didn't want to look like a mama's boy. He told us of how he threw away the cassava on his way, only to get hungry and regret his actions.

Dad would tell us many stories and we would laugh together. We had a lot to learn from him and his experiences. He wasn't ashamed of where he came from or the mistakes he made. Instead, he made fun of his own mistakes and shared them with us. I think that he did this hoping that we would know that it's okay to make mistakes but we have to learn from them.

Shubila Ruth with parents on her first birthday

Shubila Ruth with parents at three years old

9. CHARITY WORKS

An individual has not started living until he can rise above the narrow confines of his individualistic concerns to the broader concerns of all humanity.

Martin Luther King, Jr.

SPIRITUAL ATTACK

We were finally alone in the house, a few weeks after we had buried our father. Ibrahim started going to work. And on one afternoon, it was just our helper and I in the house. I took an afternoon nap, since I still had difficulties sleeping at night. My body would give up during the daytime. Then something happened. The water truck that supplied 5,000 litres had arrived. As the motor pumped the water into our tanks, it made a lot of noise. Since my room was near the water tanks, I could hear the suppliers talking and water splashing into the tank in my state of sleep. I wanted to get up but I couldn't hold my head up. That scared me. It was as if something was pressing me down.

I called out "Jesus, Jesus". Nothing happened.

Then I said, "I will do good."

Then suddenly, I was able to wake up from the position I was sleeping.

For months, I didn't tell to anybody about this. First of all, I thought people wouldn't take it seriously considering that I had just lost my dad. Secondly, I was scared of the energy it would create. As a principle, I never talk about negative things or events because I feel talking about them will give them life. As a result, I was scared to sleep. My mind was constantly occupied with thoughts of death. I couldn't tell Deo who was my boyfriend at the time. I was not even sure that our relationship was what God wanted. I was keeping my distance from him while seeking God's direction on the matter. This was a difficult time.

After I had suffered the attack, I was occupied with thoughts of death all the time. Even when I set off on a journey back to school, and also months after I had arrived in Wuhan. I read a lot to run away from my mind while in Tanzania. I would read different books and the Bible almost all the time I was awake. When I got back to Wuhan, I was fortunate enough to have a good friend and a young sister, Brenda to stay with me. We slept in the same bed and we spent most of the time together. That gave me some comfort but I was still thinking about the attack I had.

What Did It Mean To Do Good?

I read the Bible to find out what it means to do good. I felt like I was given a second chance or a warning to do good in my life. I thought this could be my mind playing tricks on me, maybe I was just exhausted when that bizarre thing happened. On the other hand or it could truly be a message from God for me to do better with my life. Either way, I couldn't really take chances and ignore this if it was truly a message from God.

I concluded was that doing good meant turning away from evil [1 Peter 3:11], being a better person, and choosing to do right instead of wrong [Deuteronomy 6:18, Romans 2:6-7]. It meant more than just obeying the Ten Commandments. It meant having a profound fellowship with God. According to Hebrews 13:16 |NIV, *and do not forget to do good and to share with others, for with such sacrifices God is pleased.* Doing good also meant charity.

Upon my return to Wuhan, I heard of a fellow student who needed financial assistance to treat a rare cancer infection. Before this fellow student, I had never involved myself in any charity. I also hadn't gotten involved in any cancer initiatives – although there were times when I would get convicted that I needed to get involved somehow. It's like I had closed that part of my life and getting involved would open it all up.

Deciding and getting involved to help this fellow student was scary. I didn't know him before. I had just read his story on a friend's social media page. I prayed for God's strength and direction. Later on, a thousand wristbands were printed for the "No One Fights Alone" charity. My friend Brenda, my fiancé Deogratius and I joined forces and bought a couple of them which we then sold. We got enormous support from the Wuhan community. We raised more than 59,000 RMB. It was three times more than our highest expectation. At the end it was more than the money but the love and support that was shown to our fellow student. We thank God for His grace and how He touched people to contribute.

We had three music events to support this; a classical music night, and two nights of international and local performance. We also joined a street sale where we sold the wristbands and organized a street basketball game. Lastly, we went door to door, selling wristbands in the dorms of different universities in Wuhan. We wanted to get more people involved in showing love and support. We also wanted God's name to be glorified as we helped this fellow student.

SOUL CONVICTION

My soul was conflicted whenever alcohol was involved in the Charity events. I tried to get less involved with organizing the last music event but wasn't possible. And my photo ended up on the wall of the lounge and bar where we held the charity event. When I saw this, I laughed at myself, "Give the devil a finger and he will take the whole arm." Finally, I got enough strength to tell people that alcohol shouldn't be served. I managed to make this a reality, alcohol was not sold at the street basketball game, which was our last Charity event. People didn't receive this well. It was normal to have alcohol in such games, it contributed to an energised atmosphere. The vendors explained that selling alcohol meant more funds collected for the cause. But the conviction inside me was too strong. I was in a time of prayer and fasting a few days before the game, and I bumped into the word that says *obedience is better than fasting* [1 Samuel 15:22 | NLT]

While putting up posters for the charity game, I met a few male friends and I told them that there would be no alcohol at the coming game. They were surprised and wondered why this was decided since they saw me on Wechat – a famous social media platform in china – drinking wine. I simply told them that I am allowed to change. And when you learn better you should do better. In the heat of the discussion, my ex who was amongst the guys there spoke out, "But you used to smoke weed" – in front of the other guys. It was something that I had told him in secret. I was able to remain calm because I had already agreed with myself that I would disclose this fact. It wasn't a secret anymore. When you decide to change you should expect confusion from your peers, especially if they are still doing the same things that you have decided not to do anymore. They might feel that you are pretending to be better than them. You shouldn't be discouraged. Keep your eyes on the prize.

Indeed, in this charity event, we collected the least money from selling snacks and wristbands. But it felt good to obey God. Although we had some worldly music that wouldn't be pleasing to God, it was a good start and a seed was planted. I was determined that the future charity events would be better. They would bring glory to God and not grieve the Holy Spirit – something that would not be expected from a believer.

A few months after 'No one fights alone' charity, I learnt about a special school in Wuhan that catered for kids affected by Autism. Some friends of mine and I decided to spend a day with them, snacking and playing. Although most of the kids had gone back to their homes to celebrate the Chinese New Year, we were able to bless and cheer up the ones that were there. We brought them school items, toys, snacks and milk as per their teacher's directions.

This charity visit was different. Although we didn't publicize it, we took photos for personal keep. A discussion was raised amongst us during this visit. Was it right to post the pictures on social media or not? This incident taught us that according to the word (cited below), our charitable deeds are supposed to only be seen by God and not advertising when we do charity.

> *"Take heed that you do not do your charitable deeds before men, to be seen by them. Otherwise you have no reward from your Father in heaven. Therefore, when you do a charitable deed, do not sound a trumpet before you as the hypocrites do in the synagogues and in the streets, that they may have glory from men. Assuredly, I say to you, they have their reward. But when you do a charitable deed, do not let your left hand know what your right hand is doing, that your charitable deed may be in secret; and your Father who sees in secret will Himself reward you openly.* [Matthew 6:1-4 | NKJV]

We reflected on this verse a little more and we felt that you wouldn't take photos of something that is considered a secret. No one will know and that's when you will receive full blown blessings for your good will.

But there are instances when you are calling out on the community to donate and raise money for a certain charitable cause like what happened with 'No one fights alone' Charity. In such circumstances, you have no way but to reveal what you want to do. We also referred to the word below that in those cases your charitable deeds would and should glorify God.

> *"You are the light of the world. A city that is set on a hill cannot be hidden. Nor do they light a lamp and put it under a basket, but on a lampstand, and it gives light to all who are in the house. Let your light so shine before men, that they may see your good works and glorify your Father in heaven.* [Matthew 5:14-16 | NKJV]

IDEAS ON PHILANTHROPY

Before China I had never involved myself in charity of any kind or thought that I wanted to. I always thought that charitable organisation had something fishy from how the media portrayed them. And this is rightly so because many of these organizations embezzle money away from projects that would help the beneficiaries. This is the picture I had of charity activities.

During the 'No One Fights Alone' charity I found myself standing in the same position of *fishy* charity organisers. Sometimes I found myself getting a side eye or questions. *Why are you really doing this? Is all the money going to the intended person?*

At that moment I felt the need to close my eyes to these suggestive accusations. I felt it's really hard for people in this industry, dealing with the urge of constantly proving themselves and fighting off dishonesty claims. But then again someone has to do this job. There are always people who are in need of a helping hand.

I applaud people or organisations that feed, cloth, educate one to millions of people. The world needs more of these men and women.

In whatever you do you will get criticism. One thing that should be important to you is to make sure that you are in tune with what God has placed in your heart. If it is in charitable deeds then go ahead and do so. You should know that your reward awaits you not from men but from Him.

10. ITS NOT ENOUGH, THIS IS ENOUGH!

If you're alive, there's a purpose for your life.

Rick Warren

NEW VENTURES

During the semester after I got engaged, in March 2016, my boss at the English Institution called me to say they missed me and there was a job vacancy. I could go back to teaching there if I had time and if I was still interested. And the truth of the matter was I badly needed an increase in my income. I would soon need to support myself if the Chinese scholarship council didn't support me, since I had asked for a yearlong extension to complete my PhD.

The day Laoshi called, I was eating rice, beans and *dagaa* (sardine) which I had brought from Tanzania. I had a lot of these in my suitcase to an extent that an Airport official in Tanzania asked for a bribe, since allegedly, the National Resources Department had to authorise such an amount of fish being exported. It was about 5 kilos. I didn't bribe him. I told him that I didn't have Tanzanian money. I thought to myself - this guy is a huge risk taker in a country that just had a new president who is uncovering corruption in different sectors each coming day. Tanzania had just elected the fifth term government under President John Pombe Magufuli in October 2015.

Anyways, back to my story. Beans and *dagaa* was all the food I had at the time. I had spent my side money buying a plane ticket that was unplanned for after missing my train in Shanghai. I didn't want to miss a meeting with my students in preparation of a scheduled teacher's audit at the university. Also, my monthly allowance hadn't been processed by the university for two months, leaving me broke. Plus, I was still experiencing the financial aftermath of traveling to Tanzania and the engagement preparations. I had no money and huge expenses coming ahead.

On the day the teacher called, my engagement ring was stolen in my dormitory as I took it off to go shower – but that's another story. This was another expense that I had to deal with. I couldn't tell my fiancé about it. I knew where he bought it and I wanted to replace it before I told him. It wasn't cheap; I knew it would take months to come up with the amount.

Laoshi complemented me in all the good things that he knew would hit home. I laughed after listening to his audio messages. I said to myself – this guy is a very intelligent businessman. I asked myself, why now? Well, after his explanation, he had about four foreign teachers and seemed to be doing well for the five months since I quit. What changed was; I had started teaching a new batch of students in my International Marketing course at the university. There were about eight students that also attended his education centre in those classes. Chinese live and breathe on guanxi, which is roughly translated as 'connections' or 'relationships'. My conclusion was that laoshi wanted me as a decorative addition to his centre since I had influence over these eight students. Killing two birds with one stone – teach these students English while they benefit from developing a close relationship with me.

You remember why I left right? Classes scheduled dropping from 100 to 5 hours in a month? Yes.

Now they want me back and I could badly use the money. But when I left, I needed the money then too. I was in a dilemma. I mean, there is being passionate and being proud. In my heart, I was worried because I didn't have enough income, yet here comes a job offer. I thought no need to die hungry with pride.

I decided to negotiate with him. He wanted me to go back and just teach few classes. But I had leverage. I said that I would go back if he guaranteed agreed to pay for fixed class hours per month, which he wasn't ready to do. I didn't want to back down and go back to the same situation that I had decided to leave. I politely apologized for not accepting his offer. I thought to myself better eat *dagaa* and beans every day. If I was going to be used, it better be on my terms. Keep walking!

By all means he meant well, he is a businessman. He swallowed his pride and approached me to come back. I think highly of him and his wife. They are very good people.

Let me let you in on a little secret. I felt very powerful, in charge of the situation after declining this temptation of going back to teach there. Learn to say 'No' sometimes even to the most tempting offers. Know your worth. You are important and valuable. If someone doesn't realize that, refuse to be treated differently. It will have great effect on your self-esteem.

This is what Stephen R. Convey in his book about private victories. [9]

> *Private victory precedes public victory... Some people say you have to like yourself before you can like others... Real self-respect comes from dominion over self.*

For example, if you schedule to get up and go for a run at 6am then you should do just that. But if you break promises that you make to yourself, you gradually lose

---

[9] Stephen R. Convey, (1989) "The 7 habits of Highly Effective people" *pg 186*

respect for yourself. Self-respect leads to higher self-esteem. If you have higher self-esteem you can allow yourself to dream big and actually know you deserve it. In your journey, only you decide if you will invite distractions at what expense. You should remember that not every good thing is necessarily good for you.

Later that week I declined an offer from a brother from church that I highly respect. He wanted me to be a part of a committee for some activity he was organising but I just didn't have time. I mean, I had limited time and I had to focus. And I almost agreed because of the excitement to think that he would consider inviting me of all people. There are distractions everywhere, jobs, events, friends, social media and so on. What are you doing each day to take you to your destination? – To take you to your true purpose – The one that God designed for your life. Great leaders who influence the world do things differently. Don't be afraid to be different. That is your power.

BEING YOUR OWN BRAND

You are a brand. What does that mean? It means you have to stand for something, have values that will set you apart from the rest. You have to know what you can do and what you shouldn't. You can't do everything and be everywhere. What do you support and what don't you? What are your principles? If you have decided to be God centred then there are things you wouldn't do or places you wouldn't go, no matter what. You will operate from your principles.

Your principles don't have to be popular. In fact your beliefs or the centre where you operate from can be the most unpopular in your environment. Abstinence is one of those things. Don't be afraid to have the unpopular idea. Be your own brand. Know who you are and where you operate from and take your stand. I once supported an event and I posted it on my wall on social media. Only later to find out it was something that I wouldn't want to go myself. I deleted the post from my wall. In another occasion, I declined a request to post someone's business on my social media wall. It was something that I wouldn't want to be associated with. Be faithful to yourself. You are the most important person to yourself. Your relationship with yourself is the second most important relationship while the first being one with God. Friends might come and go but you will always have yourself around. Self-respect is very important. Having values and sticking by them, even when others don't understand will cultivate self-respect which is vital to success.

Before my fiancé and I got in a relationship, when he was looking at me from afar, he once put a comment on my photo on my Instagram. It wasn't so bad. It was polite. But in a way he was publicly drooling or flirting with me. It's just that we didn't have a relationship like that. I find it uncomfortable even insulting when you are not in a committed relationship and people can just pass and flirt with you like you are a public commodity while blocking your chances with people who would wish to be in a more serious relationship with you. I mean, it's not the reaction I want my brand to have on people. That's exactly what I told him. "I'm sorry please remove your comment, people don't talk to me like that".

Sometimes, you might get scared a little and think that I'm being rude. Nope. Know where you stand and what you allow to be passed on you or how people should treat or talk to you. By the way, that was one of the things that made my fiancé decide to come on me harder. He saw that I respected myself. Remember that, men respect women who have standards. [10]

---

[10] Steve Harvey, (2008). Act like a lady, Think like a man. Page 123

When you choose who you are, some people will get pissed at you. But you have to know that you can't get it all. You have to choose. Do you want to be 'friendly' or put boundaries and get respected for that? I advise you, respect is much better, it lasts longer. That's one of the most attractive things you can have. They might not like you but they will respect you for standing up for what you believe in.

I had a rule against posting photos of boyfriends on social media. I mean, why post photos while you don't even know if you guys will settle down together. I learnt the hard way when an ex-boyfriend posted a photo of us with friends in a club. It didn't look so bad. We were just standing, hands around each other. But I was wearing very short shorts. When we broke up, he didn't delete this photo. Although this account is not active anymore; but the photo is still there. Now, I would never know if he really forgot the password to the account or he simply didn't want to delete the photo. Either way, I have learnt my lesson. My advice is; do not take photos that will embarrass you if they put it on the screen for everybody to see, even when you are married.

Also, you have to know there are so many nice, inspiring and motivating people out there. But there is only one you. Choose who you will follow or who is going to be a friend or a business partner. If you get yoked [2 Corinthians 6:14-18] with the wrong people it can be a good recipe for dooms day – if you wish or waste of time and energy.

These are wise words from Bishop Td Jakes on 'Grace in friends' of January 2016.

There are three kinds of people in your life and it is important to know the difference

1. Confidant – this person is in your life for you. They are the ones you can trust with your heart.

2. Constituents – are there for what you are about, where you are going if they find a faster car they will leave. They are there for the destination not for you.

3. Comrades – they are there not for you, not for what you are about but because you are fighting against the same thing. They too leave as soon as the battle is over.

Jesus is careful about access. He feeds 5000, lays hands on 70, teaches 12 and figures out who are the three. If you don't know the people in your life you might feel betrayed and disappointed in your relationships simply because you didn't know the difference and you had no business treating a comrade as if they were your confidant. Learn to ask God for everything, even friends. The older I get the more I realize how important this is a conscience decision.

As part of my '2016 bolder me' campaign, I deleted the people I was following on Instagram – from 1000 to about 100 people. With limited time and unreliable VPN – Instagram is blocked in China. This many followers was difficult to manage. Most of the times, I would be the last one to see the feeds of family members or close friends because I had so many posts on my wall. Some of the days I would be so peaceful, my mind so quiet and get into social media for all of it to be blown away. I mean, why are you 'following' a woman whose posts are mostly nudes? Or another who uses foul language from beginning to the end? Most importantly, all these people you are following, how are they feeding you? How do their posts help you? Motivate you? Make you better? You have to watch out; there are only 24 hours in a day and so many distractions. Be bold, be you!

Why Not You?

The most awe inspiring celebrity in my country, to me, is a

bongo flavour musician called Diamond Platnumz. His story is unique that we can learn from. He comes from very humble beginnings. It is said that he once sold second hand clothes in the market. But through his tenacity, hard word and passion he has made it to the top list amongst the best African musicians. He is inspiring for most people in Africa because he comes from same surroundings and pushes through to excellence, wealth and fame all over the world. Diamond has sat with presidents and different nation leaders. He has won so many international music awards. He has a huge following, millions of followers on his social media from all over the world sometimes more than some big international old-timer musicians or entertainers.

I learn there is nothing important to success like a burning desire to succeed, persistence hard work and discipline. You can read more on this from *Think and Grow Rich* by Napoleon Hill. How bad do you want it? I honestly feel that some people don't want it bad enough. *Because if you do, things happen, trust me.*

Do you know how hard it is to live in slums, no education and push to become world class? This amazes me. I might not be so much of a fan for Diamond's music – which let me say is world class quality each time but more of a fan of his journey to greatness.

Some people have it better, good education, good support from family, good family name. But they never want to be world class in whatever they do; they are comfortable with mediocrity, comfortable with ordinary. Be extraordinary my friend! Because seriously, *why not?*

Don't sleep through life. Give life your all. Everyone has greatness in them. Some people never open the gifts God has given them. Do not live in fear. *For the Spirit God gave us does not make us timid, but gives us power, love and self-discipline.* [2 Timothy 1:7 | NIV] The world needs you, your community needs you! The time is now, don't wait to start tomorrow. When my father passed away I learned to do whatever needs to be done now. I was going to wait and write a book when I got older and maybe more wiser. The devils steals our greatness like that we think we have all the time in the world but we actually don't, start now!

God answers and w*hatever* you need for the project or anything you want to do let it be known to Him. Spend quiet time with Him each day and He will show you wonders. Before you do anything or get into any venture ask God first – He loves this. *Call to me and I will answer you and tell you great and unsearchable things you do not know.*

[Jeremiah 33:3 | NIV] I take them as road maps – almost like an alarm *rrrrng rrrrng* – this is not the one! Try another one! After you have gotten a go ahead from God, He prepares people to help and work with you. Be persistent of course, but don't waste time and get stuck with bitterness when people say no. *They are not the one!*

Whatever you want to do it is possible, I always tell myself, *new deals are made every day.* Don't hold back and say this has never been done before. Make it happen!

My siblings and I in December 2013
From right: Ibrahim, Nasra, Siima and myself

Dad and all his children at Siima's Bachelor Law Degree graduation ceremony

ACKNOWLEDGMENTS

My utmost gratitude goes to the almighty God, the Alpha and Omega! You are the ever present God, I say thank you, for holding my hand and reassuring me each time I felt afraid.

I'm forever grateful for the lives of my parents, for their sacrifice and dedication to moulding us to be the best we can be.

To my fiancé Deogratius, my step mother Nanda, my siblings Siima, Nasra and Ibrahim; I'm overawed for your love and moral support. I also want to greatly appreciate your contribution in proof reading and recollection of past events.

To my relatives, colleagues and friends I'm awfully humbled by your love and readiness to contribute to the promotion of this work.

To Bro. Anthony Mutua Mutiso, my humble mentor and spiritual leader; I'm truly blessed for time you devoted and guidance provided for this purpose.

ACKNOWLEDGEMENTS

I'm extremely blessed to have had a wonderful editor Esther-Karin Mngodo. I'm indebted for her enthusiasm and commitment to make this content readable to you all.

Credit for the cover photo goes to; my sister and make-up artist Edith Chituka, for her magic and beautification on me. I will always remember your kindness. To Carol Photography for his passion and professionalism. To my student Chi Cheng for his expertise in perfecting the cover photo.

To Zion Media, for the concept and design of interior and cover of the book. I cannot thank you enough for countless sleepless nights. Without forgetting OK Studio for the final touches on the cover of the book. I am overjoyed and blessed to have you as a team.

Let me sum it up by saying that I'm tremendously overwhelmed by all the help I have received. It's truly amazing how everyone has given themselves to the success of this book. I could have not done it without you guys, may God bless you all!

Signed,

Shubila Ruth Kikoko

07/7/2016